Energy Healing for your Dog and Cat

Energy Healing for your Dog and Cat

Olivia Pozzan, BVSc

Energy Healing for your Dog and Cat

Copyright © 2017 by Olivia Pozzan, BVSc

1st edition 2017

All rights reserved. Apart from any fair dealing for the purpose of review or research as permitted under the Copyright Act, no part of this book may be reproduced by any process without permission from the author.

Cover design by Tundra Gorza

Cover image used under license from Shutterstock.com

Contents

	Introduction	1
1.	What is Energy Healing?	7
2.	Chakras and Meridians	19
3.	How to detect Imbalances	36
4.	Healing Techniques	41
5.	The Professional Touch	73
6.	Optimal Health	81
7.	Practical Tips for Common Situations	95
8.	Where Science and 'Magic' meet	106
	Appendix	125
	About the Author	130
	Bibliography and Recommended Reading	131

Introduction

This book is an introduction to the world of energy healing, and an invitation to embark on a rewarding journey of discovery with your animal companion.

More than thirty years ago, when I began my career as a veterinarian, alternative healing practices were ridiculed. Today, however, as we come to a new understanding of our multi-dimensional anatomy as an energy being, therapies emphasising an holistic approach to health are widely accepted.

In the holistic view, health is the natural order of things. Disease occurs due to an imbalance of energy flow through the mind, body and soul – or spirit – of an individual. The aim of energy healing is to restore this harmonious flow of energy thus allowing the body to heal itself.

This model contrasts with the conventional medical model, which takes a bio-mechanical view, and sees disease as a purely physical assault on the body. But once we accept that thoughts and emotions also affect health, we can readily see the limitations in the current model. Treating the medical symptoms of disease may not correct the underlying energy imbalance.

Curiously, quantum physics, which views all matter (including the physical body) as vibrating energy, has paved the way for a gradual integration of science and mysticism. In this new paradigm, energy forms the basis of reality and all things in it. This concept has profound implications. Energy, in its many guises, is both the substance and the glue that binds. Our world is made of energy, and we are energetic beings without boundaries. This interconnectedness extends throughout the universe and affects our every interaction, be that with a person, an animal, a tree or a grain of sand. In the words of the 19th century English poet Francis Thompson, *Thou canst not stir a flower without troubling a star.*

My own realization of this concept was gradual, and was sparked by achieving sporting success using visualization techniques. Intrigued, and wanting to understand how thoughts and feelings could have such a profound effect on physical performance, I began a long and rewarding journey into the esoteric realm. The wealth of knowledge and truth I found in the words and teachings of many wise people opened my eyes and changed my life. As a result, my approach to veterinary medicine evolved – and continues to do so – into an ever more holistic practice.

It is important to appreciate that an holistic approach to treatment is not an 'either-or' scenario. There is no need to choose between conventional medicine and alternative therapies. Many people, and many dogs and cats, owe their

INTRODUCTION

lives to modern pharmaceuticals and invasive surgeries. The limitation of conventional medicine rests on its lack of recognition of people and animals as complex energy beings and that energy flow must be in balance to maintain a state of optimal health. Most alternative therapies and techniques are re-packaged forms of ancient healing practices that understand this concept.

When your dog or cat falls ill, I suggest you take an integrative approach to treatment. Integrative veterinary medicine is a comprehensive medical approach to pet care that combines the best of conventional medicine and complementary and alternative therapies. Follow your vet's advice. He or she has a wealth of professional medical knowledge. But as an adjunct to treatment you can also apply the energy healing techniques you will learn in this book. Giving energy healing to your animal friend is an act of love and kindness and makes full use of the strong emotional bond you share. Because love is a powerful healing force, no-one is better suited to using these techniques on your pet than you are.

As you progress through this book, you will be led to a greater understanding of the healing techniques available and how to use them.

Chapter One begins with an overview of the new paradigm rocking the world of healing and medicine, introducing a model for the subtle energy bodies and the concept of disease as a lack of integration of the mind, body and soul.

INTRODUCTION

In Chapter Two we take a closer look at the subtle energy anatomy including the meridians and, in particular, the chakras. Maintaining health and preventing disease is a matter of harmonising the flow of energy through these subtle body systems.

Chapter Three describes how to detect imbalances in the flow of energy.

Chapter Four details various energy healing modalities and techniques. You will learn how to use touch, sound, colour, crystal therapy, aromatherapy and flower essences on your animal companion.

Chapter Five explains some of the professional therapies employed by holistic (or integrative) veterinarians, such as acupuncture, homeopathy and applied kinesiology.

Chapter Six outlines a lifestyle approach to optimal health, looking at nutrition, exercise and a healthy environment as key factors in maintaining your pet's wellbeing.

In Chapter Seven you will learn practical tips and remedies for common complaints.

If you are curious to know how science supports the concept of energy healing, Chapter Eight dips into the fascinating interplay between these two realms.

I hope that reading this book will encourage you to practice these techniques for the benefit and wellbeing of the animals you care for. Bear in mind energy healing is a subtle practice and best used as a complement to, not a substitute for, conventional treatments.

Above all, no matter what treatments, methods or

INTRODUCTION

modalities you choose, your love, directed with focus and intent, is the most powerful medicine you can give your pet.

1

What is Energy Healing?

Doctors and veterinarians are skilled in diagnosing disease in the physical body and treating illnesses with a variety of pharmaceuticals. If we – or our pets – were solely physical beings, this approach would work perfectly. But, despite treatment, some illnesses persist or recur. Why?

The physical body is merely the densest part of our anatomy. We also have a non-physical component to our anatomy. It consists of a number of subtle energy bodies which surround and interpenetrate the physical. What affects one, affects the other.

When energy flow through the subtle energy anatomy is blocked or distorted, the immune system is compromised, often leading to symptoms of ill-health. In other words, disease is dis-ease, or lack of ease, in the flow of energy.

Health is the natural order of things. A body in balance is capable of preventing and healing whatever ails it. The aim of energy healing is to restore and maintain a harmonious flow of energy through the organism – human or animal – thus maintaining a healthy immune system. When the mind-body-soul complex is in balance, the body is able to heal itself.

HARMONY AND BALANCE

Ajax, a handsome grey tabby cat, watched my every move. He had stoically endured my clinical examination but had retreated into the safety of Eric's arms as soon as the chance presented. For a cat in his prime he looked terrible. He was thin, his coat unkempt. Yet his vital signs were normal and laboratory tests showed no indication of disease. Eric assured me there had been no change in Ajax's diet, environment, or daily routine. As an afterthought he mentioned that Ajax was grooming more often. As if on cue, Ajax began meticulously licking his chest and shoulders. Grooming is relaxing to a cat so it is not surprising that they will suddenly start licking their coat whenever they feel stressed or anxious. Animals are often nervous in a veterinary consulting room but why was he over-grooming at home?

After further probing Eric admitted that the home front was no longer the cosy haven it had been for most of Ajax's life. For the past few months Eric's marriage had been faltering. Sullen silences and loud arguments were a daily norm. It took some time to convince Eric that the tension in the household was affecting his cat's health.

Ajax's condition improved after Eric created a 'safe haven' for him in his favourite room, spent more time with him, and used flower essences to calm his anxiety. But it was only after Eric's marital relationship improved and harmony returned to the household that Ajax finally returned to his normal glossy-coated self.

Emotions and thoughts are powerful energies. Understanding this is the first step in understanding energy healing. Be careful what you think and feel, not only for the sake of your own health, but also for the sake of the animals in your life. Their heightened sensitivity to our moods has a profound effect on their state of health. The energy fields of people and animals sharing a household are continually overlapping and interacting. If tension or conflict exists in the home, your pets' emotional state will be affected. If this tension or unease persists for an extended time the disturbed energy flow can result in physical disease.

Like Eric, many people are not aware of this nebulous connection between a person's state of mind and their pet's physical health. But with an understanding of the subtle energy bodies the connection is obvious. Once made, this shift in perspective makes sense of the seemingly mystical field of energy healing.

CARTESIAN SCIENCE

It may seem strange to turn to science to support the 'old but new' concept of energy healing but in fact, it is quite fitting. When the 17th century French philosopher Rene Descartes agreed to leave the question of a soul, the emotions, and *anima* strictly to the Church in exchange for human bodies to dissect for scientific research, he unknowingly set the tone for mainstream modern medicine. Dissecting the spirit out of the body made natural healing techniques seem superstitious and unscientific. Although Descartes believed in a Christian God and a human soul he argued that animals, lacking language and the ability to reason, must also lack consciousness and a soul. This was good news for the Cartesian scientists, as they became known. Animals were non-sentient automatons, the perfect living model for research and experimentation. Their cries of pain during vivisection were merely reflex reactions of the physical machine and not the cries of a soul in torment.

It was a dark age for domestic animals, an age of ignorance and cruelty. We know our pets feel emotion. They show their love for us and feel our love in return. We know they can communicate. They tell us when they want company or food or attention. We know they have a soul. We see it in their eyes. Yet the Cartesian dichotomy still prevails. If birds are sentient beings how can we support the poultry industry's caged bird policy? If chimps can learn to speak how can we subject them to a lifetime of suffering in support of biomedical research?

Reclaiming the soul, the spirit – the anima – that Descartes discarded is crucial to the paradigm shift rocking the world of healing and medicine.

THE SUBTLE BODIES

The physical body is not a closed system. It is not a container housing our thoughts, emotions and feelings. Since we can see and touch and feel this body of flesh and bone, it is easy to imagine we are no more than our physical self. Instead, the body is just one more level of density in the human energy field. This energy field, or energy body, is composed of a number of subtle bodies.

The subtle bodies do not have a fixed dimension. You can't measure their height, width or depth as you can with a physical object. Rather, they are fluid dimensional, their shape and characteristics constantly changing. Furthermore, they are not distinct and separate. Energy constantly flows in and through the whole body – the physical body as well as the subtle bodies. Thoughts, emotions and feelings are energies which can be expressed through the physical body but are not confined within the illusory borders of flesh and bone.

Have you ever walked into a room and, without a word being spoken, felt the tension between two people? Have you ever had the sensation of being watched, and turned to find someone staring intently at the back of your head? In both cases interactions on an energetic level produced physical sensations. When we talk about giving out 'vibes', sensing the atmosphere, or following our 'intuition', we are describing interactions between our subtle bodies and those of others. Since we live with our pets our subtle bodies are continually interacting with their subtle bodies. No wonder we know them so well, and they us.

The following model of the subtle bodies is exactly that – a model. In the realm of fluid dimensionality, there are no absolutes. Look at a book on Eastern traditions or esoteric philosophies and you will find models with varying levels and complexities of the subtle bodies. Models are simply constructs used to understand a concept and there is no one right view. If you cut a cake into four slices or into eight slices, it doesn't alter the integrity of the cake.

The diagram below is based on the work of 19th century philosopher Rudolf Steiner and depicts a four-fold model of the subtle bodies. It is a simple yet elegant view of the energy body of both humans and animals.

In the four-fold model, the physical body is the densest layer, vibrating at the lowest frequency. Progressing up the vibrational ladder is the etheric body. It is the body of vitality and life-force and acts as the energy template for the physical body. Next is the astral body, the realm of thoughts and emotions. Vibrating with the highest frequency is the Ego or 'divine spark'.

Remember, the subtle bodies are fluid dimensional and do not exist as separate layers. Also keep in mind the analogy of slicing a cake. Gifted psychic and healer, Barbara Brennan, commonly referred to in contemporary texts on energy healing, follows a seven-layer model.

Each of these subtle energy bodies has a focal energy centre called a *chakra* (from the ancient Sanskrit word for wheel). These centres are spinning vortices of energy that act like portals or gateways through which energy enters and leaves the physical body and are important structures in the field of energy healing.

The Subtle Bodies

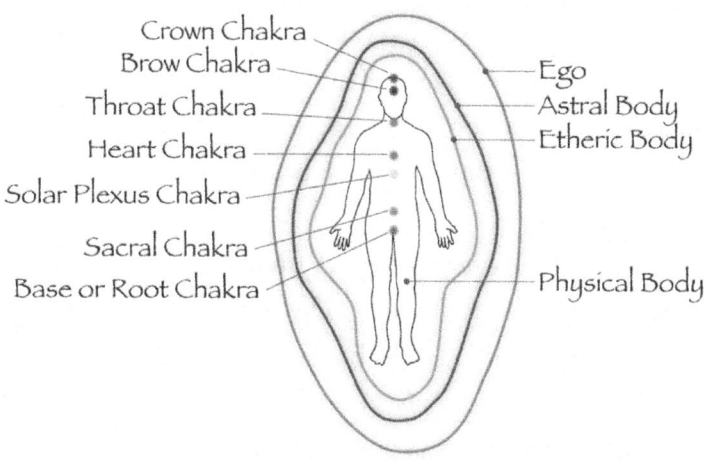

MYSTIC CATS AND PSYCHIC DOGS

Cats have enjoyed a mystical history since their first dainty steps onto the Goddess pedestal in ancient Egypt. Sometimes worshipped as a queen, sometimes maligned as a devil, the cat has nonchalantly walked the extremes of human devotion. Perhaps her dual personality – regal and haughty one moment, wild and unpredictable the next – engenders respect or fear, or both.

Dogs have had a more informal relationship with humans. As companion, watchdog, protector, shepherd and loyal friend the dog has happily settled into his allotted role in his adopted family. But sometimes, when the moon is full and he feels the call of his primeval ancestors, we realize he sees a world we cannot.

Animals have perceptive abilities far beyond our own.

What is Energy Healing?

Although dogs and cats have limited colour vision, a cat can see ten times better at night and has a field of vision 70° greater than humans. A dog can hear sound frequencies of 40 kHz (twice that of a person), and their sensitivity to certain smells is one million times greater. And their perceptive abilities go even further, well beyond the range of the physical senses.

We also have extrasensory capabilities. You may call it intuition or simply 'knowing'. This extra-ordinary sense lies in the realm of the subtle bodies. It is one way we can communicate with our pets. Recall some of your experiences and you may recognise an instance when this occurred. In the account that follows I unknowingly tuned into this sense.

Elka came to see me early one morning in tears. She had found a stray, orphan kitten and it was close to death. The kitten was a small black bundle of matted fur that barely covered the palm of my hand. She was in a terrible state. Her eyelids were crusted shut with infection, her nasal passages were so congested she could hardly breathe, ulcers pitted her tongue, and she was so weak that she fell over when she sneezed. It was one of the worst cases of cat flu I had seen. The kindest thing was to end her suffering.

Her heart pattered steadily against my fingertips as I picked up the euthanasia injection. She licked my hand. I hesitated. And then she began to purr. She was ill yet she had trust. Elka pleaded for me to save her. With some misgivings, I decided to give the tiny orphan a day's grace. I sent Elka home with medication and advice on feeding and nursing.

A day later the kitten was no worse, so Elka continued with the treatment. The following day the kitten opened her eyes, regained her appetite and never looked back. I was relieved to have given her a chance, then promptly forgot about the incident.

Some time later, I decided I wanted a cat. I had barely made the decision when I received a phone call from Elka even though I hadn't heard from her since treating the orphan kitten nearly a year before. She was moving, she said, and had found homes for all but one of her four cats. Perfect timing, I thought. It wasn't until I picked her up that I realized Sooty was the kitten I had seen a year before. At that time – and to this day – I believe Sooty had sent me a message when I held her sick little body in my hand. She had wanted to live. I had responded to her thoughts. The connection had remained and when the time was right she had sent me another message. She needed a home and had selected me as her guardian.

Coincidence and fanciful imaginings? Or telepathy and precognition?

EAST MEETS WEST

When Descartes removed the soul, and a mechanistic view of the body prevailed, traditional Western medicine treated the human body as a well-oiled machine, seeing each part and system separate and independent from every other part and system. Urologists, dermatologists, immunologists, endocrinologists, every body part specialist sees the body through different eyes. Fragmentation is a powerful filter. The body, like a car, is seen merely as the sum of its parts. Disease is the result of an attack by a physical agent on one or more of these parts. Diagnosis of disease is based on data that is measurable and quantifiable. Operating from this premise, a fire-brigade approach to treatment is logical and rational. Douse the fire where it appears. Treat the symptom.

But in this mechanistic model, treatment is often a physical assault against the offending agent – an assault that often also attacks the body part affected by disease. Undiagnosed growth? Cut it out, along with healthy tissue. Liver cancer? Radiation and chemotherapy and a host of toxic side-effects.

Western science has advanced our knowledge of diseases and has saved many lives. Scientific principles emphasize accuracy and precision in research and experimentation and this attention to detail has resulted in amazing discoveries in the fields of medicine and surgery.

But if the blueprint for the physical body lies in the energy field, whatever manifests in the physical originates first in the energy field, in our subtle bodies. Diseases such as cancer, diabetes, arthritis – whatever you can think of – appear as distortions in the energy field weeks, months and sometimes years before manifesting in the physical body.

Thoughts and emotions are powerful energies originating in our astral body. Negative thoughts and emotions distort energy flow, resulting in physical disease. Even if the symptom of the energy imbalance is cured by conventional means, the cause of the problem persists. This is one reason recurrences or 'new' illnesses will continue to develop until the energy field is balanced. Conversely, positive thoughts and emotions can have major benefits. I realized this when my athletic performance improved through focused visualization.

When your dog or cat falls ill an holistic veterinarian will employ an integrative approach to diagnosis and treatment, using a combination of conventional medicine and alternative therapies to balance energy flow. What if your vet is strictly mainstream? Vets are animal health care experts so please follow your vet's advice. Your dog's life or your cat's wellbeing may depend on it. But you can also use the energy healing techniques outlined in the following chapters. Touch, sound, light, and crystal therapy, aromatherapy and flower essences are simple yet effective techniques that anyone can learn to use on their pets. Remember, these modalities are subtle. They are not meant to be a substitute for your vet's treatment regime.

Energy healing is non-invasive and can do no harm, so you can safely use it as an aid to conventional treatment. By balancing energy flow through the mind, body and soul, the function of the immune system is restored, thus allowing the body to heal itself.

These energy healing techniques can also be used to prevent the onset of disease. By detecting and correcting energy flow in the subtle bodies before the distortion filters down to the physical body, many diseases can be prevented.

Exploring these healing therapies with your animal

companion will strengthen the bond between you and add a fascinating, new dimension to your relationship.

How to develop your energy anatomy awareness

- Rub your hands vigorously together.

- Hold your hands in front of your face, palms facing each other and about 5-6cm apart.

- With eyes softly focused, gaze into the space between your hands. Take note of any sensations on your palms.

- You may feel the etheric energy as a prickling on your palms. You may even see it as transparent swirls or streamers moving between your hands.

2

Chakras and Meridians

In the previous chapter you were introduced to the four-fold model of the subtle bodies, and the idea that health depends on a harmonious flow of energy into and through the subtle bodies as well as the physical.

In this chapter we will explore the flow of energy through the body based on two ancient and respected traditions – the chakras of the Indian yogic tradition, and the meridians of Traditional Chinese Medicine. With an understanding of energy flow through the body, healing loses its mystery.

THE HINDU SYSTEM OF CHAKRAS AND NADIS

Prevention of disease depends on maintaining a balanced energy flow through the body. In the yogic and Hindu traditions of ancient India the life-force energy (or prana) travels through vessels called nadis. In this system, highly specialised energy centres called chakras are the gateways between each and every layer of the subtle bodies.

A chakra is a spinning vortex of energy which, like a transformer, regulates energy flow through and between the physical body, the subtle bodies and the universal energy field. Chakras spin in both a clockwise and anti-clockwise direction. Yogis and mystics describe chakras as swirling whirlpools or spheres of light. Some give evocative descriptions of luminescent lotus blossoms with circling, interweaving petals that open up and close down.

There are seven major chakras located along a column of energy that extends along the body's midline from tailbone to crown. Hundreds of minor chakras can be found throughout the body, including at the joints and the palms of the hands. Energy channels called nadis connect the chakras to each other and the physical body.

The Chakras

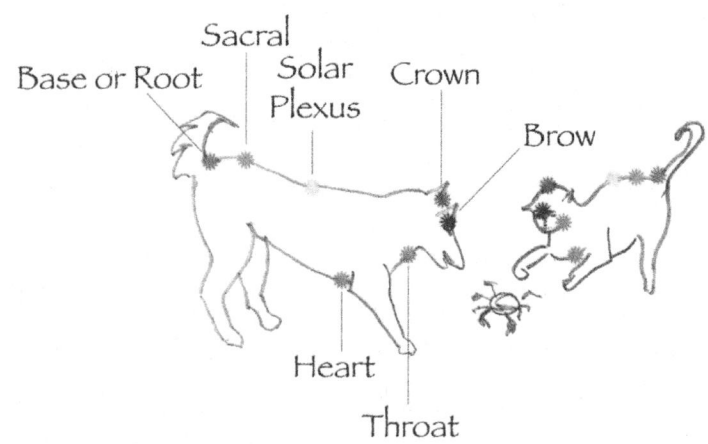

Each major chakra has a direct effect on a specific endocrine gland and the hormones it secretes, as well as on the organs and nerve plexuses in its vicinity.

Hormones secreted by the endocrine glands have a profound effect on physical, mental and emotional wellbeing. Therefore, it is easy to see that anything which interferes with energy flow through the chakras will directly affect an animals' state of being. For example, pets confined to apartment buildings and having little to do with the outside environment can develop an energy imbalance in the base chakra. This chakra is pivotal to an animal's sense of grounding or connection to the earth. The resulting imbalance can eventually manifest as a chronic skin condition.

The seven major chakras are described below.

Base or Root Chakra

In dogs and cats, the base chakra is located at the base of the tail. It governs the adrenal glands and is linked to basic survival issues. In times of stress the adrenal glands produce a surge of adrenaline which gives rise to the classic fight-or-flight response.

The base chakra connects us to the earth's stabilizing and grounding influences. When we walk in nature, lie on the grass, and anytime we are outdoors, we connect with the energy of the earth. Strong roots grow deep and like the branching roots of a massive oak, a balanced root chakra keeps us from feeling isolated and adrift.

Belonging to a tribe or community is fundamental to our nature. Social or physical isolation is a major cause of loneliness and depression and can lead to disease. Since dogs are innately pack animals, their need to belong is especially apparent.

An imbalance in the base chakra can lead to fear, defensiveness, or loss of the will to live. Other signs that could indicate an imbalance in this chakra include lower back pain, bowel and urinary problems.

To keep the base chakra balanced, ensure your pet has daily access to the outdoors. Walking on the earth, rolling on the ground, or rubbing against a tree feeds and nourishes this chakra.

Sacral Chakra

The sacral chakra is located at the sacrum – on the back in the hip region – and regulates the reproductive organs.

Through the sacral chakra our pets seek meaningful relationships with all other living creatures. As dogs tend to develop strong attachments to one particular person they run the risk of losing their sense of individualism. They are happy to be your companion on whatever excursions or hobbies take your fancy. And if you don't fancy anything physical, the emotional bond they share with you is so strong that they will ignore their own desires just to please you. This is why it is important to find out what activities inspire and delight your dog. It could be swimming at the beach or chasing a ball or running wild in the bush. Encouraging your dog to express himself through play will help maintain a healthy relationship between you.

Although working dogs have a well developed sense of purpose and a strong sense of identity, it is still important to allow them time for creative play.

Cats are far more independent than dogs and will, more often than not, do things to please themselves. But lack of attention can result in insecurity and fear of abandonment and a host of symptoms, ranging from overeating to inappropriate toileting. Ever wondered why Kitty-Kat pees on your bedspread when you go away for a few days? Disapproval, based on fear of abandonment, lies behind this unpleasant plea for attention.

Symptoms of sacral chakra imbalance overlap with those seen in base chakra imbalances and include reproductive disorders, urinary tract and bowel dysfunctions, arthritis, epilepsy, and obesity.

Solar Plexus Chakra

Located in the centre of the back, or just under the rib cage on the sternum, the solar plexus chakra is the seat of intuition, or what is often called 'gut feeling'. Animals are highly intuitive and are sensitive to your emotions and moods. How many times has your dog offered you a comforting nuzzle when you've been sad? Or your fluffy feline friend wanted to curl up on your lap and relax you with purr-therapy?

An animal's sense of self is expressed through this chakra. How well our pets can express themselves is dependent on how much freedom of expression we allow them. I'm not suggesting you let a boisterous Rottweiler jump all over your guests. Pets, like children, can and do develop bad habits. But often, when we are too busy or preoccupied with our own lives, we forget our pet's emotional needs. By ignoring a request for a pat or a belly-rub, we are sending a message that the behaviour is not welcome or appropriate. This unintentional rejection can eventually result in a pet holding onto her emotions or expressing them in an unacceptable manner. Suppressed and distorted emotions manifest as physical disease.

The close association of this chakra with the organs of digestion can result in diabetes, pancreatitis, indigestion, and gastrointestinal disorders.

An extreme example of imbalance in the solar plexus chakra can be found in those unfortunate animals that have suffered physical abuse. From years spent working in an animal shelter, I found that overly aggressive or submissive dogs often shared a history of abuse, their sense of their own power severely undermined by chronic emotional stress.

Heart Chakra

This chakra is located between the shoulder blades on the back, but its strong energy also radiates out the front of the chest between the front legs, and also between the front legs on the sternum.

The heart is the body's powerhouse. It is the cardiovascular pump that supplies oxygen and nutrients to the body's tissues and organs through the blood. You could say it is the core of the physical anatomy. Similarly, the heart chakra lies at the core of the body of energy.

As you might expect, the heart chakra is associated with the energy of unconditional love. Love is a powerful force and can have profound effects on both the giver and receiver. Anyone who has had a strong emotional bond with a pet knows the healing and stabilizing power of this love. I'm sure you have experienced this with your own pet. In medical circles, 'pet therapy' is used to help the sick and elderly. The companionship of an animal can ease feelings of loneliness and depression, can reduce a person's need for medication, can improve post-operative recovery and wound repair, and can reduce blood pressure, and many stress related disorders.

The true beauty of this emotional exchange between you and your pet is that it is reciprocal. We benefit from our pet's unconditional love for us, and they in turn benefit from our love. Love is energy. It is this energy, directed with focus and intent, that forms the basis of energy healing and chakra balancing that we will discuss in later chapters.

The thymus, an endocrine gland regulating the body's immune system, is associated with the powerful heart centre. Any auto-immune disorder, heart and lung conditions such as congestive heart failure, pneumonia, and lung cancer, as well as diseases affecting the mammary glands, the upper back and shoulders could point to an imbalance in the heart chakra.

Throat Chakra

You can feel the energy of the throat chakra on the back of the neck and over the soft part of the throat below the jaw. The throat chakra is associated with communication.

Communication is an essential tool in any relationship. We have developed a complex and eloquent language to express our thoughts, feelings and emotions, but unfortunately, we have come to rely on words as our main means of communication. Yet verbal expression is only a small part of social interaction. Body language, tone of voice, and facial expression are also important modes of communication. We subconsciously read the signs and interpret the message accordingly. However, if body language or tone of voice contradicts the spoken words, confusion often results. Have you ever received mixed signals from someone?

On the non-physical plane, thoughts, feelings and emotions convey far more information than we consciously comprehend. When you feel a rapport with a person you've just met, or conversely, if you detect tension or 'bad vibes', you've received information on a non-physical level.

This openness to communication on a non-verbal and non-physical plane is extremely important in interspecies interactions. You know when your pet is happy or sad or depressed. Some signs are obvious but others are not. In many consultations a client has told me their cat or dog 'isn't quite himself' or 'seems a bit down' without being able to point to any obvious symptoms.

Animal communicators sometimes use the analogy of tuning in to a different frequency on a radio, one where animal language is translated immediately into thoughts or images or words. Although these people have refined psychic abilities, with practice anyone can learn this subtle form of communication. For myself, it doesn't happen all the time but, especially with cats that are bewildered and frightened in the shelter, I have a strong sense of knowing what they need at that moment. It is a feeling rather than an image.

How can you hear what your pet has to say? Clear your mind and ask if he or she wishes to communicate. Trust the thoughts and images that pop into your mind. Think in images rather than words. Make a game of it. Keep it fun for both of you. Develop this skill and it will strengthen the bond between you.

As the throat chakra is associated with the thyroid glands (the regulators of body metabolism and development), imbalances include hypo-thyroidism and associated weight gain, or hyper-thyroidism with weight loss. The throat centre also governs the ear, nose and throat and may be implicated in disorders of these organs including upper respiratory tract infections, laryngitis and ear conditions.

Have you ever gone away for a few days and returned home to find your pooch has picked up a cough from the local kennel? This highly infectious, though non-fatal, upper respiratory tract infection is called 'kennel cough' because of its rapid spread through any confined dog population. Looked at energetically, stress at being separated from you has depressed his immune system and allowed a breach in the body's natural defences. Perhaps symptoms appear in the throat chakra because of the temporary block in communications.

When trying to correlate physical symptoms with a chakra imbalance, follow your intuition.

Brow Chakra

The brow chakra is located between the eyes and is sometimes referred to as the 'third eye'. This chakra is linked to the pineal gland and to the pituitary gland, the master endocrine gland which regulates the function of the body's endocrine system.

The brow chakra is associated with wisdom, intuition and extrasensory perception. Sixth sense, telepathy, paranormal and psychic abilities all fall into this realm. The perceptive and extra-sensory ability of animals has been alluded to since ancient times. Medicine-men and shamans even developed elaborate rituals and ceremonies to invoke these seemingly magical animal power qualities.

There are many recorded instances of animals predicting natural disasters, of finding their way home after a long-distance move, of predicting their owners' homecoming – no matter how irregular the person's routine. Some of these phenomena can be explained by sensitivity to the earth's electromagnetic field or to electrostatic changes in the atmosphere, or to acute hearing, or to a well developed sense of smell. But many instances are scientifically inexplicable – such as dogs and cats that can find their way home after flying inter-state to a new destination, pets that can predict medical conditions in their owners before physical disease manifests, and animals that can predict storms or natural disasters.

Have you ever had trouble finding your cat when it's time to go to the vet? Cats like a routine and can usually be found in one of their regular resting spots. So many times clients have rung me to cancel an appointment because, for some reason, their pet had sensed something was up, and disappeared. Our furry friends are smarter than we think. I once had a cat, Max, who had the uncanny ability of sensing incoming calls and would meow seconds before the phone rang.

As the pineal and pituitary glands regulate all the endocrine glands, imbalances in the brow chakra can manifest as neurological, endocrine, and immune-system disorders. Headaches, seizures and eye and ear conditions may point to blockages or disturbances in this centre.

Crown Chakra

The crown chakra is located between the ears on the crown of the head and, like the brow chakra, is traditionally linked with the pituitary and pineal glands.

The crown chakra is the gateway to higher consciousness. Through this chakra we experience unity with everything and know the interconnectedness of all. There is no 'you' and

'I'. We are all energetic beings without boundaries. Energy is both the substance and the glue that binds. The most distant star is a part of every one of our body cells. On this level, your thoughts, your body, your pet's thoughts and body, are all the same thing.

An energy imbalance in this chakra may manifest in conditions affecting the brain, head or face.

Sensing the Chakras

The Hand Scan

Wait until your pet is relaxed, either sleeping or resting comfortably.

- Sit quietly beside her.

- Take 5 deep slow breaths, consciously easing tension out of your body with each exhalation. Let your own worries and concerns dissolve.

- Think loving thoughts of your animal friend.

- When you are feeling relaxed, rub your palms together briefly, then 'scan' your dog or cat by running the palm of one hand from the base of the tail to the top of the head. You can also scan from the lower jaw down the chest and to the abdomen.

Keep your hand about 10-12cm above the body surface. If your pet allows, you can scan closer, ideally about 4-5cm above the body.

- Stop for a second or two over the corresponding anatomical locations of the chakras during the scan.

- Take note of any sensations or feelings you have. This could range from tingling in the palms, warm or cold sensations in the hands, a vague impression or image that suddenly comes to mind. It might even be a colour or sound. (I feel a prickling in my palms when I scan, as though pins and needles are lightly pricking my skin. When I pause above a chakra I feel a cloud of energy swirling against my palm. This flow feels similar to the gentle pressure you feel when you hold your hand in a bathtub full of water beneath an open faucet).

- If at first you don't feel anything, don't try harder. Engaging the analytical left brain won't help and in fact will most likely prove a hindrance. Instead, mentally thank your animal companion for her cooperation and acknowledge that on some level you were aware of the subtle energy dynamics of this interaction. The more you practice this exercise the more you will 'tune in' to the vibrations and

> frequencies of our energy world and the energetic anatomy of all living beings.

TRADITIONAL CHINESE MEDICINE AND THE MERIDIANS

As above, so below. Traditional Chinese Medicine (TCM) is an elegant system that sees the microcosm in the macrocosm. In other words, the elements and rhythms of the body are seen to correspond with those of the natural world. Originating in China over 2000 years ago, TCM employs a lyrical language which reflects the rural and seasonal lifestyle of that time.

In this system the life-force, or *chi*, flows through the body in invisible energy channels known as meridians. The acupuncture-meridian system is found in the etheric body. Acupuncture points or acu-points on the physical body are access points to this flow of chi.

TCM physicians recognize many different forms of chi, the duality of yin and yang, and the relationship of the five elements of air, water, fire, earth and metal. Unlike a Western doctor, a TCM physician does not diagnose a disease but instead looks for patterns of disharmony in the body.

There are 14 main meridian channels in the body and, similar to the ancient Indian system of nadis and chakras, each meridian is related to a major organ or physiological system. Although the meridians bear the name of a particular organ don't be misled into thinking imbalances in energy flow will only show signs of dysfunction in that organ. If energy flow through a meridian is blocked or distorted, pain or dysfunction can occur in the muscles, organs, nerves or glands anywhere along that meridian pathway. For example, the stomach meridian runs the length of the body from just below the eye to the end of the second toe. This meridian-organ link explains why a stomach upset can be associated with knee pain.

Sensing the Meridians

Just as you can 'feel' the chakras using the hand scan technique described in the table above, you can also 'feel' the meridians. After rubbing your palms together, move your hand slowly over the meridian pathways about 4-5cm above the surface of the body. Become aware of feelings of vibration in your palm or in the space between your hand and your pet's body. With practice you will discern changes in this vibration and will even be able to detect a flowing movement along the pathway.

Of the 14 meridians, two flow along the body's midline. The conception vessel runs along the ventral midline from the perineum to the lower lip and is the most yin of the yin meridians. The governing vessel runs from the nasal philtrum (the line extending from the upper lip to the nose), over the head, and along the back to a point just under the tail. It is the most yang of the yang meridians.

Of the 12 organ meridians, there are 6 yin and 6 yang meridians. Energy flows through alternating yin and yang meridians in a smooth continuous movement. In the yin meridians energy flows from the chest down the inside of the forelimbs to the paws, and from the inside of the hindlimbs back to the chest. In the yang meridians energy flows from the outside of the forelimbs up to the chest and head, and from the head down the body and the outside of the hindlimbs to the paws. When scanning the meridians, start anywhere along the meridian wheel and follow the flow of energy as it moves in the following direction through the meridians: lung, large intestine, stomach, spleen, heart, small intestine, bladder, kidney, pericardium, triple heater, gall bladder, and liver. The meridians are paired (left and right) so remember to scan both sides of the body.

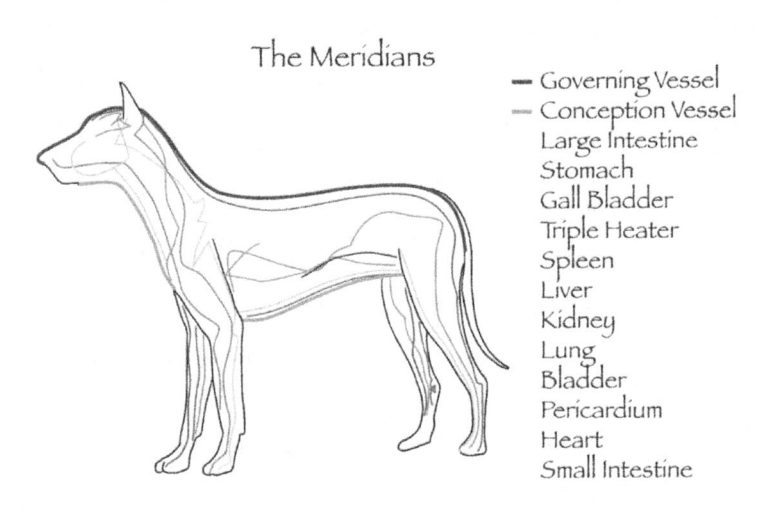

The Meridians

— Governing Vessel
— Conception Vessel
Large Intestine
Stomach
Gall Bladder
Triple Heater
Spleen
Liver
Kidney
Lung
Bladder
Pericardium
Heart
Small Intestine

Acupuncture is a form of therapy that restores energy flow and balance through the meridians. A skilled practitioner will insert needles along the meridian pathways to stimulate or calm energy flow. Although acupuncture is a specialised skill, you can help maintain a balanced energy flow through the body by simply moving your hand along each meridian channel. When you move your hand along a meridian you are flushing energy through the channel.

Acupressure, where you apply finger pressure to acupuncture points along these pathways, can also stimulate, unblock or reset energy flow.

Re-set your body clock

Each of the 12 organ meridians dominates the energy wheel for a two-hour period over a 24-hour cycle. If you've ever suffered jet lag, an easy way to re-set your body clock is to run the meridian pathway that corresponds with the time of day of your arrival. For example, the heart meridian is energy-dominant between 11am and 1pm. If you arrive at your destination during this time, run your hands along the heart meridian pathway a few times. You will effectively re-set your body clock to the new time zone and minimize the effects of jet lag.

3

How to detect Imbalances

In conventional medicine, diagnosing disease is a process of collating and assessing information, tying together the presenting symptoms with results from blood tests, x-rays, CT scans and more. Once a diagnosis has been made, treatment focuses on alleviating symptoms and treating the physical problem. But you now know that disease isn't always due to a purely physical cause. Sometimes it is. A broken leg resulting from a car accident is a straightforward case. But where a disease has an underlying energetic imbalance this must be addressed for the body to reach a state of optimal health.

So how can you determine if there is a distortion in the flow of energy in your pet's subtle bodies? The simplest technique for checking energy flow is the hand scan described in the previous chapter. Scan the chakras and the meridian pathways then scan all over the body. Look out for areas of heat, cold, or any area of increased or decreased vibration.

If your pet is suffering from a specific complaint, the organ or body part affected will help you determine which chakra or meridian pathway is out of balance. For example, if your dog has kidney problems, the sacral or base chakras may be out of balance. If your cat has pneumonia, you might suspect an imbalance in the heart chakra. An animal with a sore elbow could have blocked energy in the triple heater meridian.

Another way of checking the vitality of the chakras is through dowsing.

Chakra Dowsing

- Construct a pendulum. You can use a favourite crystal hanging on a chain, a ribbon threaded through a ring, or a wooden peg on a piece of string.

- Wait until your dog or cat is resting quietly. Make yourself comfortable beside her. Suspend the pendulum over the general area of the chakra, approx 4–5cm above the body.

- If the chakra is vital and balanced, the pendulum will swing in either a clockwise or anti-clockwise circle. The circumference of the circle indicates the strength of the chakra.

- If the pendulum movement is sluggish, it could indicate an underactive chakra. A fast swing could indicate an overactive chakra.

- If the pendulum remains stationary or if the pendulum swings back and forth or in an elliptical pattern instead of in a circle, look for physical symptoms of illness in that chakra's related organs and glands.

Dowsing is best performed along the spinal column as some animals feel uncomfortable, vulnerable, or threatened when they lie on their backs. Never force an animal into a position. Your pet should be comfortable and relaxed when you test the chakras.

ENERGY TUNE-UPS

Even in the absence of physical symptoms you can assess the vitality of each individual chakra and use the techniques described in the next chapter to prevent disease from manifesting in the body. Likewise, when an unusual spot is found on a meridian pathway, you can restore energy flow by running your hand along the meridian as though flushing energy through the channel. These energy tune-ups are quick, easy and fun to do for both you and your animal friend.

To work with your dog or cat on a deeper level, practice communicating and, more importantly, listening. Pick a quiet time when he or she is resting, and follow the instructions below.

How to listen to your dog or cat

- Close your eyes and take 5 deep, slow breaths. With each in-breath, sink into your heart.

- Visualize a warm golden light flowing out from your heart centre.

- Let this light flow towards your dog or cat. Let the light fill both your hearts and radiate through your bodies. See it as a golden halo cocooning you both together. Stay in this place for as long as you like.

- When you are ready, and with your heart and mind open and connected, invite your pet to talk.

- You may hear or see or sense words, images or sensations. Explore the experience. If you feel upset or sad or feel a sudden pain in a leg or arm, could your dog be feeling those emotions or pains? Do memories of special moments with your cat flow

> into your mind? Do you see colours? Are they bright or dull? Are they localized over a certain body part? Don't dismiss anything.
>
> - If your dog has communicated an illness or your cat revealed an upset, ask how you can help. Assure her that you will help if you can, and send thoughts of love and comfort.
>
> - Whenever you communicate on this level, always end the session by sending a golden stream of loving energy and thanks to your pet.

Due to the strong interaction of your thoughts and emotions on your animal friend's energy body, whenever you dowse, scan, tune-in, or perform energy healing, work with focus and intent.

Of course, if your dog or cat is ill, follow the advice of your veterinarian and use any medication he has prescribed. Integrating both conventional treatments and energy healing techniques has the greatest benefit for your pet's wellbeing.

4

Healing Techniques

Energy healing recognizes the body's natural tendency towards health and vitality. Balancing energy flow through the physical and subtle bodies allows the organism – human or animal – to heal itself. This is a crucial point in energy healing. Remember, health or illness merely reflects what is occurring in the invisible realm of the subtle bodies. The aim of energy healing is not to treat the symptoms of disease but to correct the flow of energy in the subtle bodies.

Everyone and everything is interconnected. Have you ever sensed that your cat was a bit off-colour or that your dog just wasn't himself even though you couldn't pinpoint what exactly triggered this feeling? How many times has that vague feeling proved prophetic when a week or two later your pet developed definite symptoms of ill-health? Remember Ajax and Eric in an earlier chapter? The subtle bodies of each animal and every person in a household are continually interacting. Without conscious awareness, the intuitive person will respond to a distorted energy flow – dis-ease – in their animal companion. Recognizing this interaction on a practical level allows you to be directly involved in the healing and recovery of your four-legged friend.

To examine all the various complementary and alternative therapies available today is beyond the scope of this book. In this chapter you will learn the following energy healing modalities and techniques that are easy and simple to use on your pets.

- Touch
- Light and colour
- Sound
- Crystals and gem elixirs
- Flower essences
- Aromatherapy

Benefits of Energy Healing

The act of healing is a gift of giving but also of receiving and you will notice a boost in your own wellbeing. Energy healing...

- improves optimal health of both healer and patient.
- improves rate of wound repair and post-op recovery time.
- decreases levels of stress hormones.
- reduces pain.
- improves the effectiveness of conventional treatments.
- improves communication and the emotional bond between healer and patient.
- boosts the immune system, allowing the body to heal itself.

TOUCH: THE POWER OF HEALING HANDS

You bump your head, you automatically massage the painful spot. You have stomach pains, you instinctively rub your belly. A frightened puppy is soothed in the cradle of your arms. An emotional upset eases as you stroke and pet your cat. Touch. At a subconscious level the intent to heal and protect lies behind the simple action of placing a hand over a wound or injury. At a physiological level, blood flow to the site is increased, endorphins are released, stress-inducing cortisols are reduced, pain is diminished and the wound heals at a faster rate.

As a shelter vet, I see first-hand the beneficial effects of touch on frightened and sick animals, especially in stressed cats. Cats detest change, so to suddenly find themselves in a noisy shelter is very stressful for them. They quickly succumb to diseases such as cat flu, a debilitating respiratory infection which is prevalent in shelter environments. However, a recent study has shown that the simple act of stroking and petting cats for ten minutes, four times a day, from the day they enter the shelter has the effect of reducing outbreaks of this disease.

Hands-on-healing is the oldest form of natural therapy. Every act of touch involves a transfer of energy through minor chakras in our palms. Shaking hands, stroking a cat, rubbing your belly. In some parts of the world patting children on the head is discouraged as the transfer of energy through the palm is thought to affect the crown chakra.

Cartesian science ridiculed the non-medical healing arts as primitive folklore. Consequently, those who recognized the value of these ancient teachings were forced to pass on their knowledge through secret societies and organizations. No wonder the esoteric field became shrouded in mystery – even today it retains an air of mystique – and its concepts thought to be available only to a few. The truth is that we all have 'healing hands'.

Hands-on-healing has branched into various streams such as Tellington TTouch, Therapeutic Touch, Reiki and massage but every form of touch involves a transfer of energy. With focus and intent we can direct this energy towards healing ourselves and our pets.

Healing through Touch

- Pick a time when you and your pet are both relaxed, preferably when he is resting peacefully.

- Take 5-10 deep, slow breaths to clear your mind of your own concerns and worries. With each breath feel yourself grounding to the earth.

- Let your breathing return to a normal rhythm, and with each in-breath focus on the flow of energy entering your lungs. Visualize it as a ray of white light.

- Feel the energy flow through your body. Becoming aware of your own energy will improve your ability to feel the energy fields around you – including your pets.

- Now visualise your pet as happy and healthy. Picture a time when the two of you shared a loving moment – maybe when you played chase-the-stick at the beach with your dog or when your cat sprawled across your lap while you were reading by the fire. Capture this image. Bring it into your heart. Focusing on loving thoughts increases the coherence of your heart chakra energy.

- Gently place your hands on your pet's body. It may help to murmur her name, but do whatever feels right.

- When you are ready, ask your dog or cat for permission to give healing.

- The answer may be obvious (a gentle sigh, purring, softening of the eyes, rolling over, moving closer) – or very subtle (a vague feeling of 'yes'). If your pet moves away or seems uncomfortable, this could be an indication that the moment is not right.

- Honour the response. Don't continue if you receive signals or sensations to the contrary. Thank your pet and try again another day.

- If you perceive consent, stay relaxed throughout the treatment. Keep your mind clear of your own concerns. Focus on loving thoughts and stay alert to your dog's or cat's reaction.

- Gently run your hands over your pet's body. Start 10-12cm above the skin surface. Pause over each chakra but don't limit your scan to just these areas.

You can scan closer to the skin surface – about 1-2cm above the body – but try not to touch the skin or hair.

- Sense any areas of distorted energy or any areas that feel 'odd'. This may include areas of rigidity or resistance, hot or cold spots, light, vibrations or unusual sensations in the palms of your hands.

- Direct healing energy into these areas. Focus on and visualize the white light flowing from your palms into your pet's body. It may be easier to visualize this energy as love. You are sending love to your animal friend.

- Don't give the energy any specific directions. Rather, heal on a general level because the symptoms or sensations you experience may not be the underlying problem. Trust that this loving energy will flow to the areas that need re-balancing.

- Stop when the time feels right. Maybe your dog will stand up, your cat will move away, or you will feel a shift of some sort within yourself. Listen to the signs.

- Send silent thanks to your pet for allowing the session.

> You may not feel or sense anything during the session but directing loving energy, with focus and intent, will still have a healing benefit.

Tellington TTouch

Author and animal behaviour expert Linda Tellington-Jones has developed a gentle method of circular finger movements to use over the body to calm and soothe frightened or anxious animals, to reduce stress and tension, muscular aches and sprains, and improve circulation and wound recovery. It is a simple yet extremely effective technique.

Starting at a point anywhere on the body, use gentle finger pressure to draw a 1-2cm circle. If you imagine a clock face, start from the six o'clock position and move your fingers in a one-and-a-quarter turn to finish at the eight o'clock position. The middle finger leads the movement and the thumb trails the forefinger by a few centimetres. Then slide or move your fingers a short distance to another point on the body and repeat. Continue doing this until you have covered your pet's entire body.

There are a number of Tellington TTouch movements, the most common being the Clouded Leopard described above. Other movements include the Lying Leopard (cupping an injury with the hand and moving the entire area in a circle), and the Python Lift (lifting the skin and muscle with the hand, holding for a few seconds and gently releasing).

Gentle touch soothes and relaxes an animal but if a dog or cat is aggressive or fractious, the movements can be performed 5-6cm above the body until the animal is sufficiently pacified to accept direct touch.

Reiki

Although having its origins in the Tibetan sutras, modern Reiki was rediscovered in the 19th century by a Japanese monk and scholar, Dr Mikao Usui. Reiki is a healing technique in which the healer channels universal energy into the patient through the palms of the hands. It is not necessary to diagnose disease or imbalances in the patient nor is it necessary for the patient to understand or believe in the process. The healer sends energy and the patient's inner intelligence guides the energy to where it is needed.

Reiki healing involves the use of symbols by an attuned healer. During attunement by a master, the student concentrates on the symbols, absorbing the energetic message encoded within. Once attuned, whenever a healer uses these symbols with focus and intent, healing energy is transferred to the patient. Reiki does not require direct physical contact. Everything is interconnected. Our subtle bodies are fluid dimensional and have no boundaries. Concentrating on the Reiki symbol and thinking of the patient with loving energy will effect healing at a distance.

I have used Reiki on many of my animal patients, and

regularly on my own cats, as well as the Healing through Touch method described above. One patient who had an affinity for Reiki was Bruno, a beautiful chocolate Labrador with hip dysplasia. This painful condition causes degeneration of the hip joints and arthritis. Massaging the muscles around the hips often eases tension and pain in the area but Bruno found even the gentlest massage uncomfortable. However, when I gave him Reiki (holding my hands just above his coat) he would lie down and go to sleep. His owner, Sharon, was so impressed she decided to learn Reiki so she could give Bruno healing treatments at home. Whenever Bruno wants a session he pushes his head under her hands and directs them to his rear end. During the session he settles down on the floor and goes to sleep. When he's had enough he gets up, has a good shake, and thanks Sharon with a wet lick across her fingers.

If you are interested in learning Reiki, attend a practical workshop and obtain initiation from a Reiki Master.

Sensations during Healing

When giving a treatment you may feel

- Tingling in your palms or fingers.
- Hot or cold sensations in your hands.

- A sense of having your hand either pushed away or drawn towards your pet's body.
- Images, thoughts, or words that seem to come from somewhere, or someone, else.

In your animal friend, watch for the following signs

- A change in breathing rate. Relaxation will slow and deepen respiration.
- Yawning, softening of the eyes, and drowsiness, particularly if the session is pleasant and your animal friend feels warm and safe. She may even fall asleep.
- Muscle twitches, particularly in the legs.
- Restlessness if unpleasant or uncomfortable sensations are experienced.
- If he moves away, it is time to end the session.

Massage

No discourse on touch therapy would be complete without a word on massage. Most dogs and cats find massage a pleasurable experience, soothing and relaxing both the body and the mind.

Massage decreases blood pressure and heart rate, stimulates the lymphatic and circulatory systems, flushes toxins out of the cells, increases endorphin production, relieves anxiety and tension, improves immune system function, and generally feels good. This, in turn, improves energy flow in and through the body.

Massaging your pet is simple. Whenever you stroke your cat as she brushes up against you or pat your dog when he sits by your side, you are giving a massage. Pat, stroke, rub your fingers lightly in a circular motion or along the direction of hair growth, and you are giving your pet a deluxe treatment.

Read facial expressions and body language and you'll soon gauge the right pressure to apply. I'm sure your pets will let you know their favourite massage spots. My cat, a big brown tabby called Mac, loves having his chin rubbed. He is quite particular, insisting on slow, gentle strokes from the base of his throat to the point of his chin.

Elderly dogs suffering hip arthritis can benefit tremendously from trigger-point massage. Continual stress on the hip joints results in tight, spasming muscles around the back and rump. Applying firm digital pressure on the knot or trigger point for 5-10 seconds stimulates blood flow to the muscle. These trigger points can be quite sensitive so do be gentle. Relax and repeat two to three times.

Combined with soothing music and aromatherapy you can make massage a relaxing exercise for both you and your pet.

LIGHT AND COLOUR THERAPY

Sunlight strikes a sky full of raindrops and forms a rainbow.

White light strikes a glass prism and refracts into a spectrum of colours.

Colour is a good example of relative perspective. Rods and cones in our eyes determine what we see and how we see it. A buttercup looks yellow because it does not absorb this light frequency, it reflects it. From a different viewpoint the flower is every colour but yellow. From the prismatic perspective of a honeybee's eyes the flower is an unmistakable fluorescent ultraviolet. Understanding that we view our world through the in-built filters of our eyes and that what we see and experience is not necessarily ultimate reality helps us keep an open mind about unconventional treatments and practices.

Light is essential for health. It affects the hypothalamus, the pineal and pituitary glands and has a direct effect on the body's biorhythms. You may recall from Chapter Two that the pituitary gland controls all the endocrine glands and thus our hormonal and emotional state.

Not only does white light directly impact physical and emotional health, research has shown that different colours of light also have specific and measurable effects on mood and physiology. Red light stimulates the sympathetic nervous system and has an excitatory effect, whereas blue light stimulates the parasympathetic nervous system which calms and relaxes.

Light and colour therapy has been used as a healing modality by priests, shamans and healers throughout history. In Babylon and ancient Egypt, tombs and temples were painted with particular colours for their spiritual, healing and mystical properties. The ancient Greeks and Romans used sunlight as a healing treatment for skin conditions. Conventional medicine also uses light in the form of laser therapy in surgery and in the photodynamic treatment of some cancers. Light boxes are used to treat people suffering Seasonal Affective Disorder (SAD) in countries with long, grey and relatively sunless winters. Bright light stimulates serotonin production which has antidepressant effects.

In energy healing, colour-puncture is used to balance energy flow through the body by focusing single wavelengths of coloured light into specific reflex points along the meridians. Coloured crystals, cloths and even different coloured foods are used for their subtle energy effects.

Each of the seven major chakras vibrates at a frequency which resonates with a specific colour on the rainbow spectrum. Balancing the chakra involves the use of either the resonant colour to stimulate energy flow or its complementary colour to sedate or calm the energy flow.

How to use Colour Therapy

- An effective method is to follow the steps outlined under Healing through Touch. When you place your hand over the chakra, visualize a coloured light leaving your palm and entering your pet's body. Allow the energy of the colour to go where it needs to go.

- Another method is to place a silk or 100% cotton (not synthetic) coloured cloth over the chakra. You can also use a coloured cotton sheet to line your dog's or cat's bed.

- Place a coloured crystal in your pet's bed or hang it from a collar.

Colours of the Chakras

Select the corresponding colour to stimulate, or the complementary colour to calm, energy flow into and through the chakra.

Chakra	Corresponding Colour	Complementary Colour
Base	Red	Turquoise
Sacral	Orange	Blue
Solar Plexus	Yellow	Violet
Heart	Green	Magenta
Throat	Blue	Orange
Brow	Indigo	Gold
Crown	Violet	Yellow

SOUND THERAPY

Sound is an invisible but physical force caused by pressure waves vibrating in the air. If the rim of a crystal wine glass is flicked, producing a pure tone, and a singer vibrates the same note, the glass will shatter.

Our bodies resonate with different frequencies of sound. During relaxation or meditation the physical body vibrates at a relatively low frequency of 8-10 Hertz (Hz) which corresponds to the range of alpha and theta brainwaves.

Sound and music, especially drumming and chanting, had greater importance in the quieter world of the past. Acoustic archaeologists have shown that many sacred sites and temples were constructed so as to enhance the voice and amplify instruments used in rituals and ceremonies. The idea of sound as magic can be found in many creation myths. Some cultures believed the magical quality of music to be so potent that it could only be used in a ritualistic framework. Rhythmic drumming, especially in a shamanic context, induces trance and altered states of consciousness by driving brainwaves into the low frequency theta range.

Music can be soothing or stimulating. A mother cat purrs her kittens to sleep, a ticking clock wrapped in a blanket soothes an orphan pup. Music or sound of about 60 beats per minute decreases the heart rate, respiratory rate and electrical activity of the brain and muscles. It also increases production of the body's feel-good hormones, endorphins, and decreases the level of stress hormones. The overall effect is one of relaxation. Music with a faster beat has the opposite effect as I'm sure anybody who has walked into a nightclub can appreciate. Music with a loud throbbing beat resonates with the base and sacral chakras stimulating sexual urges and desires.

Sound below the level of hearing (below 20 Hz) is called infrasound. Wind, ocean waves, the shifting of desert sands, can all produce sounds too low for us to hear. Some animals communicate solely by infrasound. The ocean is a sea of singing fish whose songs we never hear. Through this medium whales can communicate thousands of kilometres, across an entire ocean. Elephants also use infrasound to communicate over vast distances. Although we can't hear infrasound these frequencies still affect us physiologically, psychologically and energetically.

Sound therapy is routinely used in conventional medicine. Physiotherapists use ultrasound to reduce inflammation in muscles and tendons. These high frequency, ultrasonic waves cause the tissues to vibrate at a faster rate to produce a healing effect.

Listening to soothing music is a pleasant way to de-stress. Chanting, singing and intoning mantras also generates healing vibrations in the body. We can even select sounds and music to balance each chakra. The pure single sound frequencies of a tuning fork resonate with the individual chakras and can produce profound effects. Chakra music resonates with and balances each chakra, from base chakra didgeridoo beats to heart chakra piano melodies. Try playing the appropriate music when using any chakra balancing modality.

Always be aware that a dog and cat's acute sense of hearing makes them extremely sensitive to sound. We hear frequencies up to 20,000 Hz or 20 kHz. Dogs hear frequencies up to 40 kHz. Cats, with ultrasonic hearing up to 65 kHz, can hear the clicking of a butterfly's wings. So when your cat doesn't respond when you call, you can be sure you are being ignored.

Music for the Chakras

Chakra	Instrument
Base	Drums, didgeridoo, double bass
Sacral	Viola, guitar, lute
Solar Plexus	Classical guitar, sax, trumpet
Heart	Piano, classical viola
Throat	Flute
Brow	Harp
Crown	Tibetan or crystal singing bowl

CRYSTAL THERAPY AND GEM ELIXIRS

Crystals have been valued throughout the ages as tools of divination and sorcery, trade and wealth, healing and beauty. Ancient priests and shamans revered dazzling and often bizarrely shaped natural crystals as gifts from the Gods.

Crystals are prized for their ability to store, magnify and direct vibrational energy. This quality of crystals has applications in the industrial field where quartz is used in capacitors and air purification systems and liquid crystals are used in computers, communication systems and watches. This same ability to amplify and transform energy is the reason crystals hold a special place in the world of energy healing.

Certain cellular systems within the physical body have crystalline properties. Crystals resonate with this biocrystalline network, and the vibrational frequency of the stones can be used to balance the chakras. Remember the colours corresponding to each of the chakras in the section on Colour Therapy? In general, each chakra resonates with a crystal of the same colour. It is no coincidence that belly dancers often wear ruby red stones in their navels. Stimulating the sacral and base chakras stimulates sexual desire in their audience.

When selecting a particular gemstone, follow your intuition. Pick the stone that feels right. Or close your eyes, visualize your pet, and select a stone. When using crystal therapy with focus and intent you act as a conduit, channelling healing energy into the crystal where it is magnified and directed into your pet.

If you have difficulty selecting a crystal or no particular stone presents itself, select a general energy regulator and balancer like clear quartz or amethyst. To protect and cleanse the chakras, select tourmaline or garnet. To improve the connection between yourself and your pet, use quartz.

Crystals and the Chakras

Chakra	*Crystal*
Base	Ruby, bloodstone, agate, tiger's eye, garnet, onyx, smoky quartz, red jasper
Sacral	Ruby, amber, fire opal, topaz, citrine, jaspar, moonstone, carnelian, orange calcite
Solar Plexus	Amber, topaz, malachite, yellow tourmaline, moldavite, tiger's eye, moonstone
Heart	Emerald, jade, pink tourmaline, azurite, rose quartz, green quartz, green aventurine
Throat	Sodalite, blue turquoise, blue calcite, angelite, blue kyanite, blue lace agate
Brow	Sapphire, turquoise, aquamarine, lapis lazuli, blue tourmaline, azurite, blue topaz
Crown	Amethyst, pearl, blue and white fluorite, sapphire, lapis lazuli, sodalite, moldavite

The shape of the crystal also has subtle effects. Clusters radiate energy from their many points into the environment whereas single-pointed crystals are directional, focusing energy through the point tip. Use single-points when balancing individual chakras and clusters for general work.

To maintain a clear and harmonious household environment place a large amethyst cluster in the living room. Both you and your pet will benefit from the recharged atmosphere.

Crystal Healing

- Scan your dog or cat to detect chakra imbalances using the Hand Scan technique described in Chapter Two.

- Select the crystal that resonates with the chakra to be balanced.

- Cleanse the crystal by washing it in fresh water for a few minutes and then leave it to dry in direct sunlight or moonlight for a few hours.

- There are a number of ways to rebalance the chakras with crystals:

    - Attach the crystal to your dog's collar.
    - Hold the crystal in the palm of your hand while going through the steps of Healing through Touch. Or place the crystal over the corresponding chakra while directing healing energy through the stone and into the chakra.
    - Place the crystal in your dog's bed or your cat's basket.
    - If the crystal is large, place it in your pet's favourite room.

- As with other forms of energy healing, be aware

> of sensations or indications from your animal friend regarding the appropriateness of the healing and the timing of healing.

Gem Elixirs

As with crystals, gem elixirs have been used since ancient times. Often associated with witchcraft and pagan practices, it is interesting to note that a nun in the Middle Ages, Hildegard of Bingen, is remembered for her many gem elixir recipes.

Gem elixirs are simple and easy to make. First cleanse the crystal by washing it in fresh or running water for a few minutes then allow it to dry in sunlight or moonlight. After cleansing, place the crystal in a glass of water in direct sunlight for a few hours before removing the stone. The vibrational energy of the crystal will be imprinted in the water.

Gem elixirs can be stored in a dark glass jar in the fridge for up to one week. A daily dose of two teaspoons can be administered in the food or water or directly onto the tongue. The energy absorbed in this fashion resonates with and balances the corresponding chakra and thus has an affect on its associated physical organs.

To preserve the elixir for a longer period, mix it with 50%

brandy and store in a dark glass dropper jar. Use only a few drops of this preserved elixir in your pet's food or water.

As a guide, aquamarine is a useful elixir for any healing work, agate can lighten the mood of a long-faced pooch, while fluorite's antiviral properties make it a popular remedy to use alongside conventional treatments for viral infections.

Crystals for Common Complaints

Agate	Depression
Azurite	Arthritis
Aquamarine	General healing
Calcite	Skeletal problems
Fluorite	Antiviral
Jade	Geriatric conditions
Lapis lazuli	Respiratory problems
Lodestone	Pain
Obsidian	Infections
Rose quartz	General healing
Snowy quartz	Loneliness
Yellow topaz	Coping with transitions (like moving house)

FLOWER ESSENCES

Throughout history, plants have been used for their medicinal properties. Traditional herbal remedies and the shamanic 'jungle juices' of the Amazonian rainforest are potent medicines. By analysing these properties, the pharmaceutical industry has produced analogous synthetic drugs. In essence, the root of present day pharmaceuticals can be said to lie in herbal folklore.

Every aspect of a plant can be used in healing. Even a flower, a plant's most beautiful creative expression, has special therapeutic properties.

The legendary civilizations of Atlantis and Lemuria were said to use flower essences in healing but modern-day usage begins less than a century ago. In the early 1900s, Dr Edward Bach, a holistically-inclined bacteriologist, discovered that wetting his lips with early morning dewdrops from flowers growing in direct sunlight calmed his emotional state. Following his intuition that emotional imbalances cause disease, he set out to analyse which flowers affected and balanced various emotional states. From his studies he developed what have now become known as the Bach Flower Remedies.

Flowers are the highest vibrational aspect of a plant. By soaking a flower in a glass of fresh spring water and leaving it in direct sunlight the water takes on the vibrational imprint of the flower. As with other forms of energy healing modalities, flower essences resonate with the higher vibrations of the subtle bodies to balance energy flow.

Since Dr Bach first wet his lips with flower dew, more and more essences have been developed, from the flowers of the Texan deserts to the Australian bush, from the orchids of the Amazon rainforest to the Himalayan valleys.

A standard combination of five flower essences (Star of

Bethlehem, Cherry Plum, Impatiens, Clematis and Rock Rose) also known as Dr Bach's Rescue Remedy is a useful first-line treatment in cases of traumatic shock. Red Chestnut will help calm a dog suffering separation anxiety. Walnut will ease the emotional upheaval of moving house.

Flower Essences to balance the Chakras

Chakra	Flower Essence
Base	Red Grevillea, She-Oak, Boab, Clematis
Sacral	Red Grevillea, She-Oak, Wild Rose, Crab apple, Elm
Solar Plexus	Gentian, Five Corners, Wild Potato Bush, Hornbeam, Larch
Heart	Waratah, Monga Waratah, Angelsword, Sturt Desert Pea, Sturt Desert Rose, Heather
Throat	Old Man Banksia, Wild Oat
Brow	Banksia Robur, Impatiens, Cerato, Olive
Crown	Old Man Banksia, Angelsword, Sydney Rose, Cerato, Olive

There are a number of ways you can administer flower essences. You can add the essence to her drinking water, massage it into her skin or mix it in her food. These essences are extremely safe and can be administered a few times a day. Due to the close emotional bond between you and your animal companion it is highly likely she is reflecting your own energy imbalance. If this is the case you may consider taking the essence as well.

An easy way to dose both yourself and your pet is to rub the essence on her gums with your finger.

Make your own Flower Essences

- Sterilize a glass bowl with boiling water then let it air dry.

- Fill the bowl with pure spring water.

- Pick the flower in the morning while the petals are still covered in dew.

- Handling the flower as little as possible, place it in the bowl of water. Although one flower is enough to make the essence, if possible pick 3 or 4 flowers to cover the surface of the water.

- Leave the bowl in direct sunlight for 3 hours.

- Don't use your fingers to remove the flowers from the bowl. If possible, use twigs or branches from the same plant to pluck them out of the water.

- Pour the water into a dark coloured storage jar half-filled with brandy. This is the Mother Tincture.

- Add 2 drops of the Mother Tincture to a 30ml dropper bottle filled with equal proportions of brandy and spring water.

- Use 4-5 drops of this stock solution in food or drinking water. Or rub the essence across your pet's gums with your finger. (Shake the solution well before use).

Turn to the Appendix at the back of this book for a list of Bach Flower Remedies and Australian Bush Flower Essences to use for common emotional or behavioural conditions your dog or cat may experience.

AROMATHERAPY

For thousands of years, both cosmetically and therapeutically, essential oils have been used to anoint the human body. Egyptian priests embalmed their pharaohs and Roman beauties perfumed their bodies. In the East, pleasant aromas were seen to enhance energy flow in the body by encouraging a deeper, slower breathing rate while in Europe essential oils were routinely used as medications.

Essential oils are extracted from the flowers, leaves, seeds, resin and bark of aromatic plants and trees. Various methods, including compression and steam distillation, are used to extract the oil. When using essential oils for healing purposes it is important to use the pure oil and not a synthetic fragrance oil.

Like touch, sight and sound, smell is another portal of perception. The vibrating molecules of an aroma are absorbed through the mucous membranes of the nose and have a direct effect on the olfactory centre of the brain. The olfactory centre is located in the limbic region, the emotion-mediating area of the brain. Different aromas evoke different emotional responses and consequently produce a range of physiological effects on the body. Essential oils are particularly useful when treating emotional and behavioural upsets.

Although essential oils are often used in dogs, cats are another matter. Cats lack a liver enzyme necessary to detoxify the terpenoids in essential oils. Pennyroyal, white willow and tea tree oil, for example, can be dangerous and even fatal in cats. A cat's heightened sensitivity to essential oils even extends to the use of oil burners. Do not use oil burners in a cat household. Inhaling certain aromas can do your cat more harm than good. Until the effects of aromatherapy on cats is fully known and understood, use these potent potions only under the supervision of a skilled aromatherapist or an holistic veterinarian. Your canine friend, however, with a sense of smell far superior to your own, will find aromatherapy a potent energy balancing therapy.

When selecting oils, it is important to understand that what is suitable to use on people may not be suitable for animals. Substituting remedies between species can prove harmful. Some oils are contraindicated during pregnancy or lactation (in both humans and animals). Sage, wintergreen and wormword are neurotoxic; clove and mustard cause skin irritation, and undiluted cinnamon bark oil should never be applied directly to the skin. Essential oils can also interfere with the action of homeopathic remedies. Be aware of these complex interactions and, if possible, seek the advice of a veterinarian experienced in aromatherapy.

Keep these essential oils in your medicine kit

Cats are sensitive to essential oils. Do not use these products on your cat.

Chamomile: soothes aching muscles and burns, and is also used to treat dermatitis.

Eucalyptus: for bronchitis, sinusitis and other respiratory problems.

Frankincense: boosts the immune system and calms anxious animals.

Oregano: an antibacterial useful to treat any infective process.

Lemon: works as an insect repellent as well as boosting the immune system.

> **Peppermint:** for nausea and motion sickness.
>
> **Sandalwood:** antibacterial, antiviral, antifungal, antidepressant.
>
> **Evening primrose:** eczema.
>
> **Lavender:** antidepressant, antibacterial, insecticidal, sedative, pain, burns.
>
> **Neroli:** antidepressant, chronic diarrhoea.
>
> **Rosemary:** pain, respiratory problems.
>
> **Tea tree:** antibacterial, antifungal, antiviral, anti-inflammatory, insecticidal, and stimulates the immune system.
>
> (from *Aromatic Medicine for Veterinarians* by Dr Tonia Werchon)

Essential oils can be administered in a number of ways. Heating the selected oil in an oil burner creates a pleasant, aromatic ambience in the home for you and your canine companion. But you can also massage the oil into the skin behind the ears where she can't lick it off. Never use the neat, or undiluted, oil on your dog's skin unless you have first sought professional advice. Instead, add 3-5 drops of the essential oil to 10mls of a carrier oil such as olive, jojoba or almond oil. When dosing, take into account the size of the dog. A Chihuahua might only need one drop of the blend whereas a Great Dane can handle 5-6 drops.

And remember, essential oils should never be administered internally. Do not add them to food or drinking water.

Aromatherapy Blends for Common Conditions in Dogs

Arthritis

To 25ml of carrier oil, add the following essential oils:

- Eucalyptus 2 drops
- Wintergreen 2 drops
- Lavender 5 drops
- Rosemary 3 drops
- Black pepper 1 drop

Apply 1-3 drops to two large joints or along the spine. Use daily for 4 days then decrease frequency of application.

Flea wash

To 300ml of any gentle shampoo or castile soap add:

- Lavender 10 drops
- Eucalyptus 5 drops

- Rosemary 5 drops
- Cajeput 5 drops
- Pennyroyal 5 drops

Calming Blend

Use this blend in dogs suffering distress from thunderstorms, or in any situation that causes anxiety. To 30ml of carrier oil, add 3 drops each of:

- Lavender
- Valerian
- Marjoram
- Neroli

Dab 1-6 drops (depending on the size of the dog) behind the ears.

(from *Aromatic Medicine for Veterinarians* by Dr Tonia Werchon)

5

The Professional Touch

Some energy healing modalities require the services of a skilled practitioner and I encourage you to seek the advice and expertise of a veterinarian who has undertaken specialised training in these areas. Acupuncture, for example, requires a functional understanding of Traditional Chinese Medicine (TCM), the meridian system and the location of the acupuncture points in the body. A vet who practices integrative medicine may also employ herbal medicine, chiropractic, nutraceuticals and other treatments not covered in this book.

TCM AND ACUPUNCTURE

Originating in China over 2000 years ago, TCM is a complex system in which a physician looks for patterns of disharmony in the context of the animal's life and environment. When you visit a veterinarian who practices TCM, she will pay close attention to body shape and constitution, ask you detailed questions on what your dog or cat likes and dislikes, observe the appearance of the tongue, qualities of the 12 pulse points, breathing patterns, behaviours and body odours. She may talk of damp, heat, cold or wind in the organs. TCM is an art as well as a science, a dance of dualities, of yin and yang, and the relationship of the five elements, eight principles, the vital essences and fundamental textures. Restoring balance to the system may involve acupuncture, food therapy, herbal remedies, exercise or a combination of these.

As a form of therapy, acupuncture is effective in treating disease and maintaining health. It involves the insertion of needles into the acupuncture points along the meridians or into non-meridian acu-points to balance energy flow through the system. It is particularly effective in the treatment of spinal conditions, musculoskeletal disorders, and in the management of chronic pain. It is also used to treat seizures, allergies, digestive system disorders, behavioural problems, and an impressively long list of health complaints. On a physiological level, acupuncture has been found to stimulate endorphin release, increase blood supply to the tissues, remove toxins, improve lymph drainage, improve immune system function, and relieve muscle spasms.

Although acupuncture needles should only be inserted by a skilled acupuncturist, acupressure (where finger pressure is used in place of needles) is a simple technique you can easily learn. Your veterinarian may show you the correct technique and relevant acupressure points to use on your animal as part of your pet's home-therapy.

The following account by holistic veterinarian Dr Linda King demonstrates the power of TCM and acupuncture.

> When Hugo, a 13 year old Golden Retriever, suffered a seizure one morning, his owner, Sarah, raced him to an emergency clinic. Sarah was distraught. Hugo's eyes were rolled back in his head, both his front legs were stiff and trembling, and he was unable to rise. By the time Sarah reached the emergency clinic, Hugo's fit had passed.
>
> After a second fit soon after, Hugo was referred to a veterinary specialist centre but neither blood tests nor an MRI showed any significant findings. It was assumed that Hugo had suffered a stroke.
>
> Sarah wanted Hugo to be as comfortable as possible and to enjoy his remaining time with her family. She decided to take him to a veterinary acupuncturist.
>
> For the first six weeks of treatment, Hugo received weekly acupuncture sessions. He was placed on a new diet based on good quality low-grain, home-cooked meals. He was also treated with Chinese herbs. Sarah learned how to give Hugo daily heat therapy, moxa and massage. Gradually, Hugo's shaky legs were strong enough for short daily walks. Acupuncture sessions were scaled back to once a month but he continued on this treatment regime.
>
> Hugo did not suffer another fit. His quality of life was maintained, and even improved. He lived happily for another six months before passing away peacefully in his sleep.

If you have an interest in TCM, acupuncture and acupressure

you will find *Four Paws, Five Elements: A Guide to Chinese Medicine for Cats and Dogs* by Cheryl Schwartz DVM, an excellent text with detailed descriptions and diagrams of the meridians and acupuncture points for easy reference.

APPLIED KINESIOLOGY

Applied Kinesiology (AK) is a blending of East and West. Developed by a chiropractor, Dr George Goodheart, in the late 1960s, it applies western physical therapy to the principles of Traditional Chinese Medicine (TCM). The basic principle of AK rests on muscle monitoring, a natural feedback system using an indicator muscle to provide information on the integrity of energy flow through the acupuncture-meridian system.

In a standard assessment the patient holds one arm extended, perpendicular to the body. When the tester gently pushes down on the arm the patient should be able to resist the pressure. The muscle is said to lock and indicates a healthy flow of energy through the meridian. If the muscle unlocks (ie the patient is unable to resist the gentle pressure), the meridian has an energy imbalance. Due to the organ-meridian link, muscle monitoring different muscles can test the state of the 14 meridians.

To overcome the obvious limitation when dealing with animals, a surrogate is used. When a person touches the animal to be tested, a circuit is created, allowing the tester to monitor the animals response through the surrogate person.

But the beauty of AK goes beyond assessing the state of

the meridians. It can also be used to test which therapy the body needs, which flower essence or essential oil to use, and even what foods or substances are beneficial or detrimental to health. It is a system which you can easily perform on your animal friend. Again using a surrogate, place the substance (eg a flower essence) to be tested on your cat's or dog's body or have the surrogate hold the bottle in their free hand. If a previously unlocking muscle now locks it means the flower essence will benefit your pet. If there is no change in the response, move on to another essence – or another substance or therapy.

When I was studying kinesiology, my instructor's black Labrador, Tiger, would often sit in on our lessons. A normally placid dog, he was terrified of thunderstorms. One afternoon when thunder rumbled across the sky, he began shaking and cowering and was obviously distressed. Using the surrogate technique described above we tested Tiger for the appropriate therapy. We tested for homeopathy, aromatherapy, and flower essences. Muscle monitoring indicated his system wanted flower essences and further testing indicated a positive response to Rescue Remedy. After dosing, he settled down at our feet and we were able to continue our lesson.

With a little practice you can use this method to test the effects of different foods, music, therapies, activities, whatever you can think of, (even the effects of specific people) on your pet's subtle bodies.

HOMEOPATHY

In the early 1800s, a German doctor, Samuel Hahnemann, discovered that the anti-malarial drug quinine actually produced malaria-like symptoms in healthy people. After further investigation he came to the conclusion that, unlike conventional medicine, one of the underlying principles of homeopathy is that 'like cures like'. Symptoms are treated by dosing with a specially prepared solution that produces similar but weaker effects. A good example is belladonna, or deadly nightshade. This toxic plant produces fever, abdominal cramps, vomiting, dry mouth, headaches, earaches, and violent behaviour. As a homeopathic remedy, however, it is used to treat fevers, ear infections and aggression.

Homeopathic remedies are prepared from solutions of various plant, animal and mineral extracts that have undergone an intense dilution process. Surprisingly, the weaker the homeopathic solution, the more potent its effects. Ultimately, the most potent remedy carries only the energy imprint of the original substance. In essence, the energetic imprint of the molecules is the active healing ingredient.

Homeopathic remedies require careful storage and handling. They can be easily de-potentized and rendered ineffective by strong smells, certain foods, electromagnetic fields, and temperature extremes. Since they are safe to use and the same remedies can be used in both people and animals, you can buy a homeopathic first-aid kit to use in the household. However, a homeopathic veterinarian has undergone extensive study in this area and has the experience necessary to assess whether to treat one or all presenting symptoms, the appropriate remedy or remedies to use, the potency required for treatment, the frequency and length of administration of the remedy, and when (or if) to change the dosage or remedy. Working closely with your veterinarian in this field will better serve and assist the wellbeing, health and healing of your animal friend.

The following case notes from holistic veterinarian Dr Tonia Werchon shows how potent these therapies can be.

> Spice, a 6 year old Cairn Terrier, was suddenly struck down with hind quarter paralysis. She had no deep pain sensation, and no bladder control. An x-ray revealed damage to her lumbar vertebrae. This vertebral damage had caused demyelinization of spinal nerve roots. An operation to relieve the pressure on her spinal cord was performed immediately.
>
> Two weeks after the operation Spice was still paralysed and had also lost bowel control. The veterinary specialist who performed the operation advised euthanasia.
>
> That was when Spice's owners consulted me for treatment based on homeopathy, acupuncture, and Bowen therapy (a non invasive muscle release technique consisting of a series of gentle cross fibre moves).
>
> One month after starting homeopathic treatment and weekly Bowen therapy sessions, Spice was able to stand. Once weekly laser acupuncture treatments began, Spice took her first tentative steps.
>
> Chakra dowsing before the acupuncture sessions showed a chaotic swing over the lumbar area (indicating an energy imbalance in the sacral chakra). After treatment, dowsing

showed strong and equal swings over all the chakras – indicating they were balanced.

By conventional standards Spice should not have recovered. But six months after being told she would never walk again, she was running in the park.

6

Optimal Health

Health is not merely the absence of illness. Optimal health is a system in balance. As guardian and caregiver, you have complete control of your dog's and your cat's environment including nutrition and fitness. An holistic lifestyle, emphasising an integration of mind, body and soul, lays the foundation for a lifetime of vibrant wellbeing and is the best preventative health care you can make for your pet. Then, if illness does strike, the integrity of energy flow will be more easily restored and the body able to draw on its own innate healing power to heal itself.

NUTRITION

Food is a drug. Like any drug, the effects can be beneficial or detrimental to health. Raw, organic foods provide vital energy which enhances physical functioning. Unfortunately, poor quality commercial pet foods, often of questionable nutritional value, have become a cultural norm in our society. Many of these diets contain chemicals, preservatives, additives and artificial colours and over the long-term can cause disease. Many veterinarians consider nutritional stress to be one of the primary causes of disease, responsible for chronic allergies and many of the degenerative conditions associated with ageing.

Food provides the energy necessary for repairing and rebuilding cellular components. Cells are continually replaced throughout life. The puppy chewing your ankle today will have a completely different set of cells in his body to the old dog napping at your feet tomorrow. What he eats between now and then will have a direct bearing on his life-time health and happiness.

In the wild state dogs and cats ate raw meat, bones, and pre-digested grains and vegetables from the stomachs of their prey. As pets they often eat dry biscuits or canned food consisting of low-grade meat, abattoir by-products (powdered hooves, horns, hair, poultry feathers, beaks, feet, and animal waste), excess sugar and salt, and a host of additives, preservatives and artificial colourings. Many of the ingredients used in pet foods such as ethoxyquin, BHT, propylene glycol and sodium nitrite are carcinogenic and have been implicated in heart disease, kidney and liver failure, birth deformities, auto-immune diseases, and even certain feline anaemias. Cases of chronic skin dermatitis, asthma and disorders of the gastrointestinal tract have been linked to the chemical additives in commercial foods.

In the long term, cats and dogs fed a poor quality diet will suffer chronic nutritional stress. Years of accumulated toxins, nutritional deficiencies and immune system dysfunction considerably shortens an animal's lifespan.

Fortunately, it is possible to find nutritious commercial pet foods made from organic products. Read the label before you buy. Professional diets are also readily available. These have been formulated by nutritional scientists and veterinarians to provide all the nutritional requirements your pet needs. Sometimes veterinarians will prescribe therapeutic diets to assist in the treatment of specific disease conditions such as diabetes, heart disease or renal disease. These diets can markedly improve an animal's health and quality of life.

Ideally, to keep your pets in optimal health, feed them a wholesome diet made from fresh organic produce. Home-made diets made with fresh foods also supply natural antioxidants to combat tissue damage from free radicals. Clear eyes, shining coat, and boundless energy are indicators of a healthy diet. However, when changing to home-made it is important to meet your pet's dietary macro- and micro-nutrient requirements. Some mineral and vitamin deficiencies, especially zinc and vitamin A deficiency, can be a problem. Organ meats such as liver and kidney are good sources of vitamin A but quantities must be monitored as excess amounts will cause toxicity. Feeding your cats and dogs too many eggs is also not advisable as raw egg white can lead to a biotin deficiency. And I would recommend that you soft boil eggs, rather than feed them raw, to reduce the risk of salmonella contamination.

> **Wholesome, nutritious and home-made diet for your Cat**
>
> - Protein: 80-90% of the diet. Sources include meat, chicken, turkey, fish and eggs. Be aware that a diet high in raw fish can lead to thiamine (vit B1) deficiency.
>
> - Grains and vegetables: no greater than 10% of the diet.
> Some grains you can use include barley, brown rice, pasta or oat bran. Most cats will eat grated or finely chopped raw or lightly cooked vegetables mixed into their meal.
>
> - Supplements are necessary to replace nutrients lost due to intensive agricultural practices, storage and cooking. Add:
>
>   ○ Multivitamin-mineral mix containing Vit B complex and Vit E
>
>   ○ Fish or vegetable oil: ½-1 teaspoon per day for an average adult cat

- Bonemeal or calcium powder (dosage varies with age and stage of life).

• Once or twice a week feed your cat raw chicken necks and wings. The gnawing and chewing action will help to keep teeth clean and free from tartar.

Sample Diet

1/2 kg minced or diced chicken
1 soft-boiled egg
1/2–1 cup water
50gm boiled rice (optional)
1–2 fish oil capsules (dissolved in warm water)
1 tsp iodised salt
1 tsp multivitamin powder or 1 crushed tablet
1 tsp bonemeal

Mix all ingredients together. Divide into small one-meal ready portions. Keep frozen and thaw as required.

In recent years the question of whether or not to feed grains to dogs and cats has become a contentious issue. Allergies and intolerance to fed grains can result in skin conditions, ear infections, and inflammatory bowel disease. Some vets advocate a grain-free diet. However, the issue is a bit more complex than simply whether or not to feed grains.

Grains, vegetables and plant-based material comprise the carbohydrate portion of an animal's diet. In the natural state, cats and dogs ate pre-digested grains and plant matter from the stomach of their prey. Processed pet food, instead, has a very high cereal content which is simply refined starch. The nutritional value of the grain is damaged during the refinement process. These cereal flours are used as cheap fillers to bulk out the food. In effect, the nutritional value of the diet is compromised and the percentage of refined sugar (cheap carbohydrate) in the diet is increased. This can certainly cause problems but it does not mean that feeding grain is bad for your pet. Rather, the quality and quantity of grains, and total carbohydrates in the diet, is of greater consideration.

In general, the carbohydrate percentage of commercial dry foods is higher than either dogs or cats require.

Cats have special dietary needs as they are obligate carnivores, which means they must eat meat to survive. They cannot produce one of the essential amino acids, taurine, which is found only in animal protein sources. Cats also need a supply of linoleic and arachidonic acids which are found in animal fats. Their requirement for carbohydrate is minimal – less than 10% of their dietary intake – yet many commercial cat foods have carbohydrate contents of 40% or more. Over time, this excess (and usually poor quality) carbohydrate can lead to problems such as obesity, diabetes, skin allergies and urinary tract diseases.

Dogs are not pure carnivores, they can and will eat a variety of fruit, vegetables and grains. Just be sure to feed a diet containing high quality complex carbohydrates and with grains that are unprocessed, cracked or crushed, and pre-fermented. An important point to mention here is that dogs and cats cannot digest whole grains. They must be soaked or partially cooked to make them digestible.

To make home-made meals for your dog or cat follow the guidelines given but consult your veterinarian to determine your pet's specific calorie requirements and for advice on quality and digestibility of various food sources. Different breeds, different ages, different stages of growth (including pregnancy and lactation) means your dog or cat may require different proportions of these macro and micro-nutrients.

Wholesome, nutritious and home-made diet for your Dog

- Protein: 20-50% of the diet depending on breed and stage of life. Sources are the same as for your cat.

- Vegetables and grains: 50-60% of the diet.
  Dogs will eat vegetables and grains with more gusto than a cat, but remember to cook all grains. They also like fruit. Foods to avoid (in both dogs and cats):

  ○ grapes (or raisins), as these can cause renal failure

- onions, as the thiosulphate destroys red blood cells and can cause haemolytic anaemia

• Supplements to add:

  - Multivitamin-mineral mix
  - Fish or vegetable oil: ½ tablespoon per day for a 20kg adult
  - Bonemeal or calcium tablets or powder (dosage varies with age, breed, stage of life, and if bones are fed regularly).

• Once a week give your dog a big raw beef bone. The gnawing action will keep teeth clean. Don't allow him to keep the bone for several days. Throw it away after a day of chewing. Raw chicken wings and necks are fine to feed a small breed dog, and will help with dental hygiene.

• Avoid fish bones and never give your dog or cat cooked bones of any description. Cooking makes the bone brittle and more likely to splinter and puncture the oesophagus, stomach or bowel. The bones can also break into chunks too large to digest and result in constipation or bowel obstruction.

> **Sample Diet**
>
> 2 cups diced meat or chicken
> 2 cups boiled rice or pasta
> 2 cups cooked vegetables
> 1-3 fish oil capsules
> 1-2 tsp multivitamin powder or 1-2 crushed tablets
> 1-3 tsp bonemeal
>
> Serve in appropriate portion sizes for your breed of dog.

Variety is the spice of life. Even animals tire of the same food day after day. But a drastic change in diet might not be appreciated. Cats, in particular, don't like sudden changes in their routine. Introduce the new diet gradually by initially replacing only one-quarter of the meal with the new food. Over a period of one to two weeks increase the ratio of the new food until the transition is complete. The gradual change-over allows the intestinal bacterial flora to adjust and reduces the likelihood of dietary diarrhoea.

EXERCISE

The benefits of exercise are ingrained in us from an early age yet obesity is prevalent in our society. A person who lives on fast food and overindulges on cakes and sweets is unlikely to feel motivated to exercise. Taking the dog for a walk suddenly becomes hard work. Instead, a treat might be given to pacify a restless pooch. Unfortunately, this attitude has led to an alarming increase in the rate of animal obesity. Inactive and overweight dogs and cats are more likely to develop conditions such as diabetes, heart disease, pancreatitis, digestive disorders and arthritis. Their mental health also suffers, leading to boredom, depression, stress and anxiety.

On a physiological level, exercise increases heart rate and respiratory rate, pumps blood and oxygen to the muscles and tissues, stimulates lymph flow, removes toxic metabolites, lubricates joints, strengthens ligaments, and increases growth hormone production. Growth hormone is an anti-ageing hormone that prevents osteoporosis, loss of lean body mass and mental acuity, and promotes fat mobilization and metabolism. The endorphins produced reduce pain and stress and further enhance the physical benefits of exercise. As well as creating a sense of wellbeing, blocked or stagnant energy is shifted to restore a healthy flow of energy through the entire system.

Unless you live on acreage and your dog can run to his heart's content, a long morning and evening walk (or at least 20-30 minutes of moderate to vigorous exercise daily) will help keep your pet in optimal health. Of course, exercise intensity and duration depends on the breed, size and age of your dog. Discuss any questions or concerns you may have with your veterinarian. As an expert on animal health care she will be happy to discuss all areas of health management with you.

Dogs are great walking and jogging companions and a

good reason for you to exercise and enjoy the same health benefits. If you can't keep up with your pet's canine antics, you can throw a ball or a stick to get her heart and muscles pumping. Exercising on the beach or in a mountain forest exposes both of you to mood elevating negative ions and provides that vital connection to nature. This grounds the base chakra and gives an animal a sense of tribal belonging and security. If the great outdoors are too far away, the local dog park will give your pooch a great active and social outing.

Cats also need to exercise. If they have outdoor access they usually amuse themselves but house-bound cats need stimulation. Simple toys, such as a feather tied to a string and dragged across the floor, can provide hours of amusement. Catnip-filled toys and scratching posts are also a great idea. Be creative and have fun.

ENVIRONMENT

By controlling many of the variables that contribute to optimal health – diet, exercise, and the home environment – you greatly influence the quality of your pet's life. Use common sense when deciding what environmental conditions you can and cannot influence. For example, when you select a dog to bring home, consider space and climatic restrictions. You wouldn't own a Great Dane if you lived in a fifth floor apartment nor would you take a Husky to live in the desert.

Shelter, hygiene and social interactions with

neighbourhood animals are also factors within your control. Every animal needs a safe, clean and sheltered place where they can rest and sleep. It could be a rug on the living room floor, a spot on the end of the bed, or a kennel in the backyard. Our pets' wild ancestors had snug, dry dens as their safe havens from predators and the elements so a domestic pet should not be left outside to endure a cold, rainy night nor suffer a hard slab of concrete as their only form of bedding.

Your pet may never have to face a wild predator but some neighbourhood animals are just as terrifying. The tom cat down the road may be your cat's worst nightmare. You don't need to hear the unnerving screams of two cats fighting to know she is under attack. Puncture wounds and abscesses are an indication that neighbourly relations are less than friendly. Stress and anxiety from constant bullying can lead to fearful behaviour, loss of appetite, or inappropriate toileting. In these situations your cat needs a safe haven she knows she can trust, and a responsible guardian who will address the problem with Tom's owners.

Not all neighbourhood animals will be hostile to your pets. Many dogs strike up friendships with other dogs living in the same area and these social interactions should be encouraged. Most communities have a dedicated day and time when dogs and their owners get together for ball games and social play in their local park.

Of growing concern to the health of both animals and people in the 21st century is the barrage of environmental pollutants in the form of smog, traffic emissions, house and garden poisons, and electromagnetic radiation. Some of these environmental hazards are within your control. Every time you wash your pet with an insecticidal flea bath, or whenever she eats pesticide sprayed grass, toxins accumulate in the kidneys, liver and fatty tissues of the body. Switching to chemical-free pesticides, insecticides and household cleaning products will decrease an animal's exposure to these poisonous substances. Of course, make a judicious and informed decision. If, for example, you live in certain parts of the world where the paralysis tick is prevalent, using a chemical-based tick prevention treatment may very well save your dog from life-threatening tick paralysis. When using chemicals is unavoidable just be sure to support his overall health in the other ways discussed in these pages.

Electromagnetic pollution, on the other hand, is an unpleasant consequence of modern-day living. Household electricity, microwaves, radio waves, television, telecommunications and computers are just some of the everyday appliances we take for granted. Yet these necessities of our age are continually subjecting us, our animals, and our global environment to electromagnetic pollution. On an energetic level, electromagnetic waves distort energy flow through the system. High voltage power lines can cause aggression, depression, constant stress and cancers. A body suffering continual stress eventually suffers adrenal gland exhaustion, hormone imbalances, and a depressed immune system.

The barrage of discordant electromagnetic waves we

produce is affecting the earth's energy field. As we are all interconnected, if the earth suffers, so do we. It would be easy to dismiss electromagnetic pollution as an environmental factor beyond our control but every individual carries the seeds of change in their every day thoughts, words and actions. The more people aware of the situation, the more chance that local change will lead to a global shift. Increasing community awareness, supporting green policies, and opting for organic or natural foods and products are ways in which an individual can slow this insidious dis-ease of the earth and all her species. Every small act towards rebalancing the earth's energy flow will help keep us all in a state of balance and optimal health.

7

Practical Tips for Common Situations

As a result of working for the RSPCA as a shelter vet, I meet many animals who, for various reasons, have ended up at the shelter. It is difficult not to take home so many of these wonderful creatures. One boy I couldn't resist was Pepper, a sprightly 13 year old brown tabby cat.

Pepper readily accepted his new home. However, Mac, my cat of six years was stressed at having a newcomer in the household. Although the introduction was gradual – with a separate room for Pepper, and limited supervised meetings – to give Mac time and space to accept the changes in his home, it was still traumatic for him. Cats are creatures of habit, and they do not like changes in their routine or home life. A new cat in the household, even one as placid and good-natured as Pepper, was too much for Mac.

Within a short time, Mac became withdrawn and

Practical Tips for Common Situations

depressed, spent less and less time at home, avoided contact, and lost his appetite until he stopped eating altogether.

To reduce Mac's anxiety levels, I placed a Feliway diffuser in the living room. This diffuser emits a scent that mimics a cat's natural facial pheromones to promote a state of wellbeing and calm. I also used Bach's Rescue Remedy flower essences in both Mac's and Pepper's water bowls. To further calm the environment I played classical music at low volume.

We began the introduction process again. With Pepper confined to the spare room, Mac started to spend more time in the home. When he allowed me to stroke and pet him, I used the Tellington TTouch Clouded Leopard massage technique, which he found soothing. Dowsing over his chakras I detected an imbalance in the solar plexus chakra. As this is the seat of an animal's personal power, it was no surprise to find an imbalance here. I added honeysuckle flower essence to his water, and used Reiki over his solar plexus to strengthen the chakra.

Gradually, as his anxiety levels decreased, he began to eat again. I continued the Reiki sessions, massages and flower essences on Mac over the next month as Pepper began to explore his new home. Eventually, Pepper was able to integrate fully into the household.

Although they may never be the best of friends, at least Mac and Pepper are able to live together harmoniously. And Mac still loves having a Clouded Leopard massage.

Just as I found flower essences, massage, Reiki, music and patience resolved conflict in my household, you will find the following tips can help you and your pet through some difficult situations.

If you follow the recommendations given please remember, do not use aromatherapy in cats. Cats lack a liver enzyme necessary to detoxify the terpenoids in essential oils.

Adopting a Shelter Dog

As a shelter vet I see many dogs adopted into loving homes. And it is always heart-warming to see them settle happily into life with their new families. But this isn't always the case. Some dogs and cats find re-homing a stressful experience.

So how do you welcome a sensitive dog into the family home?

A thorough veterinary check is the first step where your vet will discuss vaccinations, diet, and parasite control. If your refuge dog is underweight but otherwise has a clean bill of health, she could be thin due to the stress of her background circumstances and her recent shelter life. In this case, good food and a loving home will soon see her fill out in all the right places. Make sure you provide her with a safe haven of her own where she can retreat if she feels overwhelmed or stressed. It could be a cosy kennel in the backyard or a sleeping basket in a corner of the living room. Supervise any interactions with young children (a child's boisterous enthusiasm could seem frightening to a timid dog) until your latest family member knows what to expect in her new home, and what you expect of her.

With a supportive and loving environment, many

emotional scars will fade away. Some animals however, particularly adult dogs with a history of abuse and neglect, can take far longer to learn to trust again. Others who have come from a loving home but whose owners are no longer able to care for them will suffer profound grief and loss and may be hesitant to love again. If your dog is overly timid or fearful or stares sadly out the window, there are ways to help.

- **Touch**: Stroking, petting and massage are ways of building trust and forming an emotional bond between you. Be sensitive to her response – if she moves away, give her space and try again another time.

- **Flower Essences**: Rescue Remedy for extreme stress
  - centaury, cerato for timidity
  - walnut, honeysuckle for nervous animals
  - honeysuckle also for sadness and adjustments
  - aspen, larch, mimulus, rock rose for fear
  - gentian, gorse for despair
  - chicory for insecurity
  - cherry plum for panic
  - sweet chestnut for abuse victims

- **Homeopathy**: aconite for fear and anxiety
  - ignatia or Nat. mur. for grief
  - staphysagria for emotional sensitivity

- pulsatilla for separation anxiety

- **Aromatherapy:** lavender or frankincense for stress.

Thunderstorms and Panic Attacks

Some dogs find thunderstorms an extremely terrifying event. Others tremble or cower at any loud noise. Never chastise your dog when he suffers a panic attack but don't encourage this behaviour by being overly attentive and protective.

So what can you do to calm a jittery dog? She will want to be in a familiar and sheltered place. Move her bed basket into a darkened room with the curtains drawn and with soothing music played loud enough to cover the rumble of thunder. Use one of the following remedies to help her through her ordeal.

- **Behaviour modification:** Fear of thunderstorms escalates with continued exposure, so desensitisation and counter-conditioning is your best strategy. Select a time when your dog is relaxed and play (very softly) recorded music of a thunderstorm. Turn it off immediately if she becomes agitated. When she is settled re-start the music at a lower volume. If she seems okay with the noise, gradually increase the volume, always keeping the music below the fear-inducing threshold. Reward her with praise or treats when she doesn't react to the incremental increase in volume. Eventually she will become desensitised to thunderstorms and associate a reward with her new behaviour.

- **Flower Essences:** Rescue Remedy for extreme stress
  - rock rose for terror
  - aspen, larch, mimulus for fear
- **Homeopathy:** aconite for fear and anxiety
  - phosphorus for fear of loud noises
- **Aromatherapy:** clary sage for fear and anxiety
  - lavender, valerian, marjoram and neroli for thunderstorms
- **Herbal Remedy:** valerian root.

When your Animal Grieves

Dogs and cats form strong attachments to the people and animals in their lives. Dogs, in particular, have a tremendous capacity for unconditional love and can suffer profound grief when a loved one dies or leaves. If his doggy friend has passed on, or someone close has left, he'll feel lonely and depressed, and will often turn to you for comfort. Cats, too, need your support during this stressful time.

- **Touch:** One of the best things you can do is spend quality time with your grieving friend, stroking, petting and playing.
- **Flower Essences:** Rescue Remedy for extreme stress

- star-of-Bethlehem, walnut, honeysuckle for grief
- gentian for despair

- **Homeopathy:** ignatia for grief

  - pulsatilla for emotional neediness

- **Aromatherapy:** bergamot for grief

  - lavender for stress.

Separation Anxiety

If your animal chews the furniture, barks incessantly, cries constantly, or soils inside the house when you're away, she could be suffering from separation anxiety. Don't punish her. Her destructive behaviour is not a way of getting back at you, and any form of punishment could increase her anxiety. A cat's reaction to being left alone may not be as obviously destructive as a dog's but clues to watch out for include loss of appetite, hiding, sulking, and overgrooming.

So how do you save the new living room rug from ruin and yourself from the feline sulks? The first step is a visit to your vet to ensure your pet doesn't have an underlying medical condition. If her health is fine, and she has enough toys at home that boredom isn't an issue, try the methods described below. Bad habits can be difficult to correct so you might consider a consultation with an animal behaviour expert.

- **Behaviour modification:** Desensitisation and counter-conditioning is your best approach. Go through the motions of leaving home (picking up your keys, putting on your coat, opening the door) but don't leave. Get her used to the cues. When she no longer reacts to the cues, ignore her for 15 minutes before actually leaving the house for a short time. When you return don't greet her for at least 15 minutes or until she has calmed down. A good trick before you leave is to hide treats around the house (especially for cats), new toys to play with, or soft music for company. While you get your pet used to your arrival and departure routine, train her to accept visual separation from you. The following works particularly well in dogs. Place a barrier in a doorway between two rooms but in such a way that she can still see you. She will most likely whine or fret but don't remove the barrier until she falls quiet. Then let her out and praise her. (If you remove the barrier while she is noisy, you will reinforce the behaviour you are trying to change. Only reward the new behaviour). Gradually increase the distance between you, always rewarding her when she behaves calmly. Eventually, move out of her sight for increasing periods of time until she no longer frets when you're away.

- **Flower Essences:** red chestnut for separation anxiety
    - vervain for highly strung animals
    - heather for loneliness and attention-seeking behaviour

- **Homeopathy:** pulsatilla for separation anxiety
- **Aromatherapy:** frankincense for anxiety
  - lavender for stress

Arthritis and Muscle Stiffness

Old dogs who have enjoyed a long life of vigorous play often find it increasingly difficult to get out of bed, particularly on cold winter mornings. The pain of chronic arthritis can lead to muscular spasm and stiffness especially in muscles around the lumbosacral area, the hindlegs, and along the back.

Senior cats also suffer the discomfort of degenerative joint disease and arthritis. After a thorough veterinary check you may decide conventional medicine will offer your animal friend the most effective pain control and management.

Energy healing techniques for arthritis and chronic pain include:

- **Touch:** Tellington TTouch, massage and trigger point therapy (using light pressure on tender spots) will work wonders. Also massage the muscles of the upper back and shoulders which often become stiff from overuse when the hindquarters lose strength.
- **Homeopathy:** bryonia
  - Rhus tox.
  - ruta
  - arnica

- conium

- **Aromatherapy:** eucalyptus

  - wintergreen
  - lavender
  - rosemary
  - black pepper

- **Acupuncture:** Chronic pain can be managed with regular acupuncture sessions.

- **Diet:** Glucosamine or chondroitin supplements in the food will protect joint cartilage and increase joint lubrication. Omega-3 fatty acid supplements reduce joint and muscle inflammation.

- **Lifestyle:** Make sure she has a soft bed and a warm winter coat. Keep her weight reasonable to relieve stress on the hip joints. Gentle exercise such as short walks or swimming will regulate her weight as well as keep her joints mobile.

Motion Sickness

If your animal friend is prone to motion sickness, one of the following remedies may prevent a car trip turning into an ordeal.

- **Touch:** Apply light pressure on acupressure point PC6

located above the wrist and in the depression between the two tendons on the back of the front leg

- **Flower Essences:** rescue remedy
  - scleranthus
- **Homeopathy:** cocculus
- **Aromatherapy:** peppermint
- **Herbal Remedy:** ginger root extract

8

Where Science and 'Magic' meet

The gulf separating classical science from the esoteric realm has narrowed considerably in the past few decades. If you are interested in surfing the interface between these two seemingly contradictory worlds, this chapter expands on allusions and references made in the previous sections. Set out as a string of clips, we dip into the world of quantum physics, cellular biology, precognition and telepathy, and take a revolutionary view of our planet Earth.

PRECOGNITION AND TELEPATHY

We've all heard of dogs and cats who can find their way home after flying inter-state to a new destination and animals that can predict storms or natural disasters before sensitive electromagnetic and barometric instruments. Although this precognition has been regarded as a mere curiosity in most circles, Chinese seismologists take these warnings seriously when predicting earthquake activity. It seems like magic, and in a way it is. Animals are deeply connected to the earth and are finally attuned to changes in the earth's energy field.

Harder to explain are dogs and cats that can alert their owners to an impending hypoglycaemic attack, epileptic seizure or pre-cancerous state. Perhaps a dog's sensitive olfactory organ can detect certain body odours when a diabetics' blood sugar level drops but how do seizure-alert dogs (and to a lesser extent, cats) know when their owners' are about to have a fit, even when they are out of range of sight and smell? Doctors have detected pre-cancerous states in people after pet owners sought advice because their dog repeatedly sniffed and licked at normal, unblemished areas of their skin. Perhaps there is a physiological explanation for these cases involving an animal's acute sensory sensitivity, but science has yet to find it.

And what of an animal's ability to intuit when his owner will arrive home? In *Dogs That Know When Their Owners Are Coming Home*, Rupert Sheldrake cites cases where witnesses reported dogs moving to wait by the door at the exact time the dogs' owners thought about and began preparations for going home. Varied routines, unexpected delays, and vast distances did not affect the dogs' accurate ability to predict the home-coming intention. This uncanny perception goes beyond an animal's acute sensory capabilities. These psychic dogs were responding to a thought.

Precognition, telepathy and extrasensory awareness are

forms of communication and information exchange that occur on a level beyond that of the physical world.

QUANTUM PHYSICS AND THE HOLOGRAPHIC UNIVERSE

An astonishing hypothesis put forward by renowned quantum physicist David Bohm is the idea that the universe is a giant hologram. A hologram is an image created by the interference pattern of a split laser light beam where one beam is reflected off an object and the other collides with this reflected beam on a recording medium (such as film). Shining a light through this medium produces a hologram – a 3D image of the object that seems to be floating in space.

Neurophysiologist, Karl Pribram, proposed a similar theory while trying to find the area for memory-storage in the brain. During his research he found that brain injuries, strokes and even temporal lobe removal might blur memories but did not result in clearly defined partial loss of memories. He concluded that memories were not stored in localized storage areas in the brain, but rather that memories were non-localized and diffusely distributed.

One amazing aspect of holographic film is the fact that when it is cut into pieces, each piece retains the image of the whole. Compare this to photographic film. When cut into tiny pieces you only get a part of the image on each piece. Pribram found that the 'whole in each part' aspect of the holographic model made sense of memories. He and other scientists further speculated that memories are stored in the energy field outside the body. The brain is the holographic film and memories are actually holograms.

As a hologram is an illusion, the holographic model of the universe proposed by Bohm completely changes the current view of reality. In *The Holographic Universe*, Michael Talbot sums up these two scientists' radical ideas:

> Our brains mathematically construct objective reality by interpreting frequencies that are ultimately projected from another dimension, a deeper order of existence that is beyond space and time: The brain is a hologram enfolded in a holographic universe.

Our minds convert frequencies into various holographic forms that we call tree, table, apple, dog, cat and so on. But what, then, lies behind the illusion?

The implications are breathtaking. In the holographic model our physical bodies are holograms that seem to occupy a single point on the space-time continuum, and behind the hologram we are waves of energy existing in a dimension beyond the constraints of space and time. In this model the realm of the paranormal and metaphysical are easily explained – everything from telepathy to levitation, from miracles to energy healing.

The link between science and mysticism goes even further. Quantum mechanics supports the idea of the interchangeability of energy and matter – the idea that matter is energy vibrating at different frequencies. In the words of

Where Science and 'Magic' meet

Albert Einstein, *Everything is made of emptiness and form is condensed emptiness.*

The solid objects that comprise our visual world are merely dense, localized vibrating wave-particles of energy without defined limits or boundaries. To fully appreciate this concept, take a moment to feel the solidity of the seat beneath you. Now imagine that you can miniaturize yourself to the size of a subatomic particle. At this level, the seat beneath you is no longer solid. You can swim through a sea of nothingness between the vibrating wave-particles. Like passing through a cloud of smoke, you can't tell where the seat begins and where it ends. The physical object is merely the densest form of vibration perceptible to the human eye. Every solid form has layer upon layer of subtle, interpenetrating vibrational levels that exist in a dynamic and boundless state. This non-physical level is the sea of nothingness within the seat as well as an expanding band of frequencies radiating out from the seat.

Likewise, the physical body is just one level of density in a field of energy extending beyond the boundaries of flesh and bone. This is the human energy field or the realm of the subtle bodies. Every living thing has an energy field that interpenetrates, interweaves and interacts with others in a never-ending dynamic dance.

Everything is energy. You are energy, your pet is energy, and as a part of the universal energy we are all interconnected.

PICKING UP VIBES

Kirlian photography is a special technique developed by a Russian electronics engineer to photograph the bio-luminescence of an object. The images reveal a corona of beautiful starburst effects depicting what many believe is the etheric body. Using Kirlian principles, biologist Harry Oldfield developed the Kirlian Gun to produce colour visuals of scanned body parts. Because cancer cells discharge intense coronas, Kirlian photography can detect hot spots before actual growths are seen in the body. Oldfield has also developed the PIP scan which uses polycontrast interference photography to scan the energy field.

Japanese subtle energy researcher, Dr Hiroshi Motoyama, has developed the Chakra Instrument to measure the number of photons emitted from the different chakras. His findings show that highly active or 'awakened' chakras emit a greater number of photons. Motoyama has also developed the AMI (Apparatus for Meridian Identification), a device which measures energy flow through the meridians. The meridians lie close to the skin surface and emit light which can be seen using infrared photography. Like the Kirlian Gun, the AMI is a diagnostic tool that can detect pre-disease states.

THE RINGS OF GAIA

As above, so below. This Hermetic axiom is a universal law. The macrocosm is the microcosm. What we see on a small scale is a reflection of the bigger picture. This concept is portrayed on every plane of evolution from the cellular to the stellar and to realms beyond our understanding.

In Chapter One you were introduced to the four-fold model of the subtle bodies. This model is also a reflection of the nature of the universe, the solar system, and the planets. Just as we see only the coarsest vibrating aspect of ourselves, so we see only the coarsest vibrating aspect of the universe and its parts. Our planet Earth exists on the physical plane but, like us, is also built of more ethereal matters. This occult tenet dramatically alters our perception of Earth, revealing a multi-faceted relationship that goes far beyond the physical boundaries of flesh and bone, soil and stone.

To the Ancient Greeks she was the goddess Gaia but many cultures throughout history have revered the earth as a living goddess. In 1970 the British atmospheric chemist, James Lovelock, proposed the Gaia Hypothesis, viewing the earth as a self-regulating organism with the ability to adjust and regulate the biosphere and the environment to maintain a homeostatic balance.

The Gaia Hypothesis is new but the concept is old, a rediscovery of ancient lore that viewed the planet as a living, breathing organism. Our relationship to Earth is dynamic and interactive, existing on levels on and beyond the physical. Eastern philosophies have long recognized the complex interrelationship we have with the earth. Feng Shui, for example, is an ancient Chinese concept that seeks to balance the energetic forces between us and the environment. It is based on the principle that energy channels, similar to the nadis of the human body, crisscross and penetrate the earth's surface. These energy channels form an interlocking lattice around the earth described by various cultures as forming repeating patterns of circles, hoops, rings or stars. Anthropologist Bethe Hagans poetically refers to this spherical matrix as the Rings of Gaia. The intersection of these grid lines are high-energy centres. Many sacred and mystical sites including the Pyramids of Giza, the Bermuda Triangle, Mount Kalais and Macchu Picchu lie on these intersections. In the British Isles dowsing has shown these etheric grid lines (or ley lines) seem to invisibly connect Stonehenge, the churches of Glastonbury, and other centuries-old monasteries, churches and pagan monuments. These high-energy centres are the earth's chakras.

Just like the chakras in the human body, the earth chakras are vortices of energy that can be open or closed, balanced or unbalanced. Areas of geopathic stress are areas of distorted energy flow in the earth's energy grid and can eventually impact on the physical wellbeing of the earth.

Because our energy field is intimately linked with that of the earth, small fluctuations in the earth's atmosphere or electromagnetic field has a major impact on our lives. Underground streams and rivers, mineral deposits, geological faults and power cables all alter the earth's electromagnetic field, and in turn, affect our subtle bodies. It is no surprise that our psychological wellbeing has a direct link to the state of our environment. This field of study, Ecopsychology, has shown that health improves when we immerse ourselves in nature.

Conversely, health suffers when we fail to connect with the outdoors or if we live in areas of geopathic stress. Every day, in the media, we hear about global warming, climate change, unseasonal weather, freak storms and natural disasters. Pollution, mining and depletion of our natural resources all contribute to these signs of environmental imbalance. Before the electrification of the world in the 20th century, the earth was able to self-regulate and maintain a homeostatic balance but wide-spread use of radar, microwaves, electromagnetic waves and even household electricity has interfered with the earth's electromagnetic field and its ability to deal with this new, insidious, form of pollution. Depression, general malaise, emotional dysfunction, cancer and certain chronic and degenerative diseases are the result in our lives of imbalances in the earth's energy flow.

BRAIN WAVES AND ENERGY HEALING

Being in sync with nature and being in a state of energy healing are very similar experiences. In both states brain wave frequencies fall into the alpha and theta ranges. During normal everyday life, brain waves operate in the beta range of 13-30 Hertz (Hz) but during meditation and energy healing, they fall into the alpha (8-13 Hz) and theta (4-7 Hz) ranges.

The interface of alpha and theta brain wave frequencies resonates with the key frequency of the earth's Schumann waves, the extremely low frequency portion of the earth's electromagnetic field. While immersed in nature a person's brain waves are naturally drawn into harmonious synchrony with the earth's field. This is one of the reasons most people find walking on the beach or hiking in the forest brings them a sense of calmness and quiet joy.

The alpha and theta states are the gateways to altered states of consciousness. These frequencies form the bridge between the conscious and subconscious, the door to insight and wisdom. In this state, near-naked yogis can comfortably weather the extremes of freezing snowfields and blazing deserts. Some can even slow and stop their heartbeats. Children and animals operate in the alpha state nearly all the time. A cat purring is well into this state.

Just as brain waves synchronize with the earth's field, during meditation brain wave frequencies from the two hemispheres of the brain synchronize. The brain wave pattern becomes more ordered. This regular, rhythmic pattern of energy has the effect of bringing other brain waves into sync. Whenever two individuals get together, their brain waves will synchronize, both resonating with the more coherent or ordered brain wave pattern. In this way, patients of energy healers are naturally drawn into the healer's alpha or theta state. This happens regardless of the healing modality used.

BE CAREFUL WHAT YOU THINK

The idea of an energy transfer through touch and thought is not a mere nebulous hypothesis. In a study conducted by

Rollin McCraty at the Institute of HeartMath one person's electrocardiograph readings were recorded on the body surface of another. In other words, when two people hold hands or are in close proximity to each other their heart energy waves can be physically detected on the other person.

Energy transfer via thought has also been measured. An article published in the 1993 International Journal of Psychosomatics recorded data measuring the electromyographs of Therapeutic Touch recipients. This form of hands-on-healing was developed in the early 1970s by Dr Dolores Krieger, a New York University Professor of Nursing. Knowing that mainstream health professionals would ridicule the notion of 'healing hands' she repackaged the energy healing techniques she learned from Dora Kunz (a well-known clairvoyant and former president of The Theosophical Society in America) under the acceptable title Therapeutic Touch.

A Therapeutic Touch practitioner does not actually touch the patient but places his or her hands about 8-12cm above the body. The research article reported that electrical activity in the muscle (or 'muscle tension') in a person was affected by the healer's intent. A healer sending uncaring thoughts caused an increase in electrical activity of the muscle, and a tense patient. When caring, healing thoughts were sent, however, muscle tension decreased and the patient was relaxed.

What you think and how you feel has a direct effect on the people and animals in your life.

Distance Healing

We are all interconnected. Our energy fields extend beyond infinity, continually overlapping and interacting. Physical separation does not separate us on the energetic level. With focus and intent, healing is effective even from a distance.

- Pick a time when you are relaxed and won't be disturbed.

- Take 5-10 deep, slow breaths to clear your mind of your own concerns and worries. With each breath feel yourself grounding to the earth.

- Let your breathing return to a normal rhythm. Now, with each in-breath focus on the flow of energy entering your lungs. Feel it flooding your entire body.

- Feel this energy in whatever form it appears. It may be a vibration or a vague sensation. Visualize this feeling as a ray of white light.

- Now visualize your dog or your cat as content and healthy. Enhance this image. Imagine the feel of her body beneath your hands. Smell her unique scent.

- Bring the image of your animal friend into your heart.

- Now direct the white light of energy to your pet wherever she may be. Silently say her name and tell her, "I send you love and healing".

- Trust the energy will connect with your dog or cat and will be used for his or her greater good.

- When you are finished, thank your animal friend and the universal energy.

You can follow these guidelines while listening to music for the chakras, burning a coloured candle corresponding to a specific chakra, holding a resonating crystal in your hand, or simply opening yourself to universal love.

THE PHYSIOLOGY OF TOUCH

What happens on a cellular level during the physical action of touch?

Renowned psychoneuroimmunologist, Dr Candace Pert, first discovered the opiate receptor on cell membranes in the early 1970s. This led to the discovery of endorphin, the body's natural feel-good hormone, and to an on-going discovery of peptides naturally produced by the body. Because peptides carry information, often of an emotional nature, between the body and the brain, Pert poetically referred to these informational substances as the 'molecules of emotion'.

Pleasurable thoughts and sensations stimulate endorphin release. Endorphins are produced in the brain and in cells all over the body and have both analgesic (pain-killing) and euphoric (pleasure-enhancing) properties. By attaching to receptors on cell membranes in tissues and organs and to the mobile cells of the immune system, these peptides exert their effects locally and throughout the entire body. High densities of these peptide receptors are located in the limbic region of the brain, the so-called emotional centre. Even single-celled organisms produce endorphins. Most people would never consider an amoeba capable of feeling pain or having feelings. That it produces a pain-killing and pleasure-enhancing chemical raises all sorts of interesting questions.

In her book *Molecules of Emotion*, Pert recounts a visit she once had from a yogi interested to know the correlation between endorphins and the chakras. Although Pert was unfamiliar with the chakra system, she and the yogi found their respective diagrams correlated perfectly, the chakras overlapping "the two chains of nerve bundles on either side of the spinal column, each rich with many of the information-carrying peptides".

As each major chakra relates to the endocrine glands and to the hormones and peptides they produce, perhaps we can say that the chakras regulate the 'molecules of emotion'.

Touching your pet with love and affection stimulates endorphin production. This is a two-way exchange. Not only does your pet's physiology respond by pumping out these feel-good peptides, but your own body responds in kind. In both of you, blood pressure and heart rate drop, capillaries dilate and blood flow increases to the area being touched. As a result lymph drainage improves, the immune system is boosted, toxic metabolites are removed and wounds heal at a faster rate.

Touching also reduces stress. Physical and emotional stress stimulates the adrenal glands to produce adrenalin and corticosteroid hormones. Normally, once the stress has passed, the body's natural feedback loop regulates further release of these hormones. But continual stress disrupts the feedback loop and more stress hormones are produced. Eventually, white blood cell activity decreases and the thymus gland (an important immune system organ) is affected. The result is immune suppression, depression, ill-health and disease. Touching, hugging and stroking stimulates endorphin release, restores the feedback loop, and decreases production of stress hormones. How many times has a sympathetic hug soothed the anguish of hurt or sorrow or grief?

British holistic teacher and author, Dr William Bloom, goes one step further. He believes endorphins have energetic as well as physiological effects on the body. He sees tension in the body as patches of frozen emotion that block or disrupt energy flow through the system. Endorphins act physiologically to reduce tension and stress, and energetically to melt these frozen blocks. Interestingly, he links the emotional 'bliss fields' of spiritual highs and religious awe to a physiological flood of endorphins.

The beneficial effects of touch on both the physical body and the subtle bodies are considerable. In the following case notes, Dr Barbara Fougere, author of *The Pet Lover's Guide to Natural Healing for Cats and Dogs*, provides a powerful example of healing through touch. As an integrative veterinarian in a busy Sydney hospital, she uses Chinese and Western herbal medicine, acupuncture, chiropractic, nutritional medicine, and Reiki, as well as conventional veterinary medicine. In Dr Fougere's words:

> Pickles, an 11 year old Old English Sheepdog, arrived at the clinic hot, fatigued and panting. She had previously been diagnosed and treated for cancer, and her spleen removed, at another clinic. Although she had recovered from surgery, her prognosis was grave as the tumour had spread. Pickles' owners had decided against chemotherapy because, in her particular case, it could not promise a good outcome. They told me they had tried Reiki on Pickles but weren't confident in their technique.
>
> I knew palliative care was the best we could do to help Pickles. With guidance, Pickles' treatment plan consisted of a change in diet, herbal medicine, gentle exercise, and regular twenty minute Reiki sessions every day.
>
> More than two years has passed and Pickles is still alive. She is certainly living well with her cancer. The hands-on-energy work of her people calmed and soothed Pickles, and helped them through the original grief of the diagnosis. Pickles seemed to really enjoy the sessions and would flop down in front of them if they were a bit late in starting. As Pickles' condition improved, the frequency of Reiki sessions dropped to a few each week. Even so, her owners still placed their hands on her

with focus and loving intent every day. Touch was (and is) powerful medicine, not only for Pickles but for her people as well.

IN HOMEOPATHY, LESS IS MORE

One of the principles of homeopathy is that a solution of greater dilution has greater potency. In 1988 Jacques Beneviste, a former research director at the French National Institute for Health and Medical Research, published an article in the scientific magazine, *Nature,* proving this homeopathic principle. His experimental research recorded immune cells responding to highly diluted solutions of IgE antibodies. Even solutions diluted to one part in 10,120 (a dilution where no IgE molecule should be left in solution), stimulated immune cells to a greater extent than did the more concentrated solutions. From a Western medical perspective, this makes no sense at all.

Beneviste also showed that water will imprint and transfer the specific sound frequency of individual molecules. Water can act as a template, recording the frequency of in-contact molecules. Once imprinted, this solution can amplify and conduct the recorded frequency. Another body of water exposed to these recordings, or even to email attachments of these signals, can stimulate the effects of the original substance. In essence, the energetic imprint of the molecules is the active healing ingredient. Again, this makes no sense in the realm of Western science. But, using the multi-dimensional model of the subtle bodies, we understand that homeopathic remedies resonate with the higher vibrational frequencies of the non-physical body. In this realm, refined energies have greater potency.

ENERGY HEALING – THE FUTURE

We live in interesting times. Our current era is undergoing one of the greatest shifts in human thinking and understanding as we embrace the interconnectedness of every being and every single thing. An integrated view of medicine and healing is part of this revolution.

As people become more consciously aware, we will see that compassion and love towards all living things, including the Earth, is the basis of focused healing. And that makes each one of us powerful healers.

I hope that using the energy healing practices outlined in this book will strengthen the loving bond you share with your animal companion and, in turn, pave the way for an enlightened future for us all.

Appendix

Flower essences can ease an animal suffering from emotional or behavioural upsets. However, consult your vet to rule out any underlying medical conditions that may be affecting your pet's wellbeing.

A guide to the remedies and the situations in which they may assist is given in the following tables. Note that this list is by no means comprehensive.

APPENDIX

Bach Flower Remedies for Dogs and Cats

Flower Essence	Condition or Situation
Agrimony	Stress, anxiety
Aspen	Fear of unknown causes
Beech	Impatience, aggression
Centaury	Timidity
Cerato	Lack of concentration
Cherry plum	Fear, aggression
Chestnut bud	Slow learners, behavioural problems
Chicory	Possessiveness, dominance issues
Clematis	Exhaustion
Crab apple	Overgrooming
Gentian	Depression
Gorse	Grief, depression
Heather	Attention-seeking, loneliness
Holly	Aggression
Honeysuckle	Anxiety, adjusting to changes in routine
Hornbeam	Exhaustion, lethargy
Impatiens	Impatience, highly strung animals
Larch	Lacking confidence
Mimulus	Fear of loud noises
Olive	Exhaustion
Pine	Guilt
Red chestnut	Separation anxiety
Rock rose	Terror

APPENDIX

Star of Bethlehem	Shock, abuse
Sweet chestnut	Anguish
Vervain	Highly strung or nervous animal
Vine	Dominance issues
Walnut	Adapting to change (eg moving house)
White chestnut	Restlessness
Wild oat	Boredom
Wild rose	Apathy
Willow	Resentment
Rescue Remedy	Shock, any emergency

APPENDIX

Australian Bush Flower Essences

(from *Australian Bush Flower Essences* by Ian White
www.ausflowers.com.au)

Flower Essence	Condition or Situation
Emergency Stock	Panic, distress, fear
Banksia Robur	Lethargy
Boab	For abuse
Boronia	Excessive behaviour
Bottle Brush	Coping with life changes
Dog Rose	Fear, shyness, insecurity, apprehension
Flannel Flower	For dislike of being touched
Fringed Violet	Distress
Grey Spider Flower	Terror
Gymea Lily	Attention-seeking behaviour, dominance issues
Illawarra Flame Tree	Rejection
Jacaranda	Excitable or scattered behaviour
Kapok Bush	Apathy, discouragement
Little Flannel Flower	Joylessness, to encourage playfulness
Macrocarpa	Jaded, drained, worn out
Mint Bush	Confusion
Monga Waratah	Neediness, addictive personality
Mountain Devil	Anger
Mulla Mulla	Fear of flames, distress from sun and heat

APPENDIX

Old Man Banksia	Weariness, frustration
Peach-flowered Tea-tree	Boredom, hypochondria
Pink Mulla Mulla	Distrust
Red Helmet Orchid	Rebelliousness
Red Lily	Disconnection
Red Suva Frangipani	Emotional upheaval
Rough Bluebell	Manipulative behaviour
She-Oak	Inability to conceive (non-physical cause)
Sturt Desert Pea	Emotional pain, deep hurt, sadness, grief
Tal Mulla Mulla	To encourage social interaction
Tal Yellow Top	Loneliness
Waratah	Despair, to enhance survival skills
Green Essence	Emotional distress associated with intestinal and skin disorders and parasites

About the Author

Olivia Pozzan, BVSc, is an Australian veterinarian and is passionate about animal welfare. She works as a shelter vet, providing care for injured and homeless animals.

Olivia began her veterinary career on remote cattle stations in the Australian outback and in rural mixed practices. She has vetted on a camel expedition in the heart of Australia, worked for an Arabian prince in the Middle East, and has accumulated over 30 years experience treating a broad range of animals. She also volunteers her time and veterinary expertise with animal welfare groups, desexing, vaccinating and treating street dogs and cats in developing countries.

In the area of energy medicine she is a Reiki Master and has studied Touch for Health (TFH) Kinesiology. Her focus on holistic therapies and an integrative approach to veterinary medicine is based on respect and compassion for all living creatures.

She lives with two beautiful rescue cats.

Bibliography and Recommended Reading

Allegretti, Jan & Katy Sommers DVM *The Complete Holistic Dog Book* (Celestial Arts, Berkeley, California 2003)

Barnett, Libby & Maggie Chambers *Reiki Energy Medicine* (Healing Arts Press Vermont 1996)

Battaglia, Salvatore *The Enchanting Art of Aromatherapy* (The Perfect Potion, Brisbane 1988)

Brennan, Barbara *Hands of Light* (Bantam Books USA 1998)

Coates, Margrit *Hands-on-Healing for Pets* (Random House London 2003)

Collinge, William *Subtle Energy* (HarperCollins Warner Bros NY 1998)

Collings, Jillie *Life Forces* (Hodder & Stoughton Ltd New English Library Great Britain 1991)

Devereux, Paul *Stone Age Soundtracks* (Vega, London 2001)

BIBLIOGRAPHY AND RECOMMENDED READING

Fougere, Barbara *Healthy Dogs* (Hyland House Publishing Pty Ltd, Flemington, Australia, 2003)

Fougere, Barbara *The Pet Lover's Guide to Natural Healing for Cats and Dogs* (Elsevier – Health Sciences Division, Australia, 2005)

Kunz, Dora *The Aura* (Quest Singapore 1991)

Gerber, Richard MD *Vibrational Medicine for the 21st Century* (William Morrow & Co Inc NY 2000)

Gerber, Richard MD *Vibrational Medicine: New Choices for Healing Ourselves* (Bear & Company Santa Fe NM 1998)

McTaggart, Lynne *The Field* (HarperCollins London 2001)

Mercer, Patricia *Chakras* (Sterling Publishing Co Inc NY Godsfield Press 2000)

Ozaniec, Naomi *Chakras* (Element Books Ltd Boston 2000)

Pert, Candace B, PhD *Molecules of Emotion* (Touchstone NY 1999)

Pitcairn, Richard DVM PhD, Susan Hubble Pitcairn *Dr Pitcairns' Complete Guide to Natural Health for Dogs & Cats* (St Martins Press USA 1995)

Ranquet, Joan *Energy Healing for Animals* (Sounds True Inc, Louisville USA 2015)

Schoen, Allen & Susan Wynn *Complementary and Alternative Veterinary Medicine* (Mosby, 1998)

Schwartz, Cheryl DVM, Four Paws, *Five Directions: A Guide*

BIBLIOGRAPHY AND RECOMMENDED READING

to Chinese Medicine for Cats and Dogs (Celestial Arts Publishing, California 1996)

Sheldrake, Rupert *Dogs That Know When Their Owners Are Coming Home: And Other Unexplained Powers of Animals* (NY Three Rivers Press, 2000)

Stein, Diane *The Natural Remedy Book for Dogs & Cats* (The Crossing Press, Freedom California 1994)

Talbot, Michael *The Holographic Universe* (HarperCollins London 1996)

Werchon, Tonia *Aromatic Medicine for Veterinarians* (Proceedings of the AVA Conference, Australia, May 1997)

White, Ian *Australian Bush Flower Essences* (Findhorn Press Ltd, Forres UK 2008)

White, Ian *Australian Bush Flower Healing* (Transworld Publishers, Australia 1999)

Made in the USA
Coppell, TX
19 August 2020